COUNTRY POEMS

COUNTRY POEMS

COMPILED BY

Martha Hayward

AURA

This edition published in 2010
by Baker & Taylor (UK) Limited,
Bicester, Oxfordshire

ISBN: 978-1-90723-102-5
AD001477EN

Printed in China

Contents

Introduction 6

SPRING 8

SUMMER 66

AUTUMN 128

WINTER 178

Biographical Notes 236

Index of Poets 248

Index of Titles 250

Index of First Lines 253

Introduction

The aim of this compilation of poetry, inspired by nature, was to provide a country basket of delights – rural verse plucked from the lofty heights of the Arcadian idyll, the humble pastoral and the sheer burlesque. In these pages you will find some of the most loved poems in the English language, written by a myriad of both celebrated and little known poets, all of whom put pen to paper to celebrate the perennial – and sometimes uncompromising – beauty of Mother Nature.

Thus is spring's fresh-faced joy perfectly extolled in Shakespeare's description of 'daisies pied and violets blue and cuckoo-buds of yellow hue', in an excerpt from *Love's Labour's Lost*. Meanwhile, autumn's atmospheric, hazy scenes are surely never more poignantly depicted than in Keats' 'To Autumn':

> *Season of mists and mellow fruitfulness,*
> *Close bosom-friend of the maturing sun;*
> *Conspiring with him how to load and bless*
> *With fruit the wines that round the thatch-eves run;*

Beyond the literal, an enduring theme in this collection is the parallel between the four seasons and the cycle of human existence. The most joyous poems, much concerned with love and romance, are inspired by the advent of spring, while summer brings a robust sense of delight: Ella Wheeler Wilcox declares in 'Summer Song' that 'no forebodings of sorrow shall darken my skies, or shall dampen my mirth.' By autumn, a chill note enters as poems acknowledge their subject's advancing years, whilst winter is a rightful mix of numb despair and celebration, brought about by the inevitability of death and the anticipation of the cycle of life continuing, ever after, into spring:

As Flora's breath by some transforming power,
Had chang'd an icicle into a flower,

tells Anna Laetitia Barbauld in her delicate poem, 'The Snowdrop'.

Whilst most poems that follow are presented in their recognized format and spelling, a few have been reworked or tweaked to enhance the read for a modern audience. My hope is that, amongst this miscellany of the joyous, the tragic and the comi-tragic, everyone will find a few verses that strike a chord or tug at a heartstring.

Martha Hayward

I sing of brooks, of blossoms, birds, and bowers:
Of April, May, of June, and July-flowers.
I sing of May-poles, hock-carts, wassails, wakes,
Of bridegrooms, brides, and of their bridal cakes...

Spring

A Light Exists in Spring

Emily Dickinson

A light exists in spring
Not present on the year
At any other period—
When March is scarcely here

A color stands abroad
On solitary hills
That science cannot overtake,
But human nature feels.

It waits upon the lawn;
It shows the furthest tree
Upon the furthest slope we know;
It almost speaks to me.

Then, as horizons step,
Or noons report away,
Without the formula of sound,
It passes, and we stay—

A quality of loss
Affecting our content,
As trade had suddenly encroached
Upon a sacrament.

Spring in New Zealand

Hubert Church

Thou wilt come with suddenness,
Like a gull between the waves,
Or a snowdrop that doth press
Through the white shroud on the graves;
Like a love too long withheld,
That at last has over-welled.

What if we have waited long,
Brooding by the Southern Pole,
Where the towering icebergs throng,
And the inky surges roll:
What can all their terror be
When thy fond winds compass thee?

They shall blow through all the land
Fragrance of thy cloudy throne,
Underneath the rainbow spanned
Thou wilt enter in thine own,
And the glittering earth shall shine
Where thy footstep is divine.

The Blossom

William Blake

Merry, merry sparrow!
Under leaves so green
A happy blossom
Sees you, swift as arrow,
Seek your cradle narrow,
Near my bosom.
Pretty, pretty robin!
Under leaves so green
A happy blossom
Hears you sobbing, sobbing,
Pretty, pretty robin,
Near my bosom.

To an Early Daffodil

Amy Lowell

Thou yellow trumpeter of laggard Spring!
Thou herald of rich Summer's myriad flowers!
The climbing sun with new recovered powers
Does warm thee into being, through the ring
Of rich, brown earth he woos thee, makes
   thee fling
Thy green shoots up, inheriting the dowers
Of bending sky and sudden, sweeping showers,
Till ripe and blossoming thou art a thing
To make all nature glad, thou art so gay;
To fill the lonely with a joy untold;
Nodding at every gust of wind to-day,
To-morrow jewelled with raindrops.
   Always bold
To stand erect, full in the dazzling play
Of April's sun, for thou hast caught his gold.

Sonnet: The Crow

John Clare

How peaceable it seems for lonely men
To see the crow fly in the thin blue sky
Over the woods and fields, o'er level
    fen.
It speaks of villages, or cottage nigh
Behind the neighbouring woods – when
    March winds high
Tear off the branches of the huge old
    oak.
I love to see these chimney-sweeps sail by
And hear them o'er the gnarled forest
    croak,
Then sosh askew from the hid wood
    man's stroke
That in the woods their daily labours ply.
I love the sooty crow, nor would provoke
Its March day exercise of croaking joy;
I love to see it sailing to and fro
While fields, and woods and waters
spread below.

Spring Wind in London

Katherine Mansfield

I blow across the stagnant world,
I blow across the sea,
For me, the sailor's flag unfurled,
For me, the uprooted tree.
My challenge to the world is hurled;
The world must bow to me.

I drive the clouds across the sky,
I huddle them like sheep;
Merciless shepherd-dog am I
And shepherd-watch I keep.
If in the quiet vales they lie
I blow them up the steep.

Lo! In the tree-tops do I hide,
In every living thing;
On the moon's yellow wings I glide,
On the wild rose I swing;
On the sea-horse's back I ride,
And what then do I bring?

And when a little child is ill
I pause, and with my hand
I wave the window curtain's frill
That he may understand

Outside the wind is blowing still;
… It is a pleasant land.

O stranger in a foreign place,
See what I bring to you.
This rain – is tears upon your face;
I tell you – tell you true
I came from that forgotten place
Where once the wattle grew, –

All the wild sweetness of the flower
Tangled against the wall.
It was that magic, silent hour…
The branches grew so tall
They twined themselves into a bower.
The sun shown… and the fall

Of yellow blossom on the grass!
You feel that golden rain?
Both of you could not hold, alas,
(both of you tried, in vain)
A memory, stranger. So I pass…
It will not come again

The Canterbury Tales

AN EXCERPT FROM THE PROLOGUE

Geoffrey Chaucer

When that April with his showers sweet
Has pierced the drought of March to the root,
And bathed every vein in liquor of such power
By which virtue engendered is the flower,
When Zephyrus also with his sweet breath
Has quickened again in every grove and heath
Tender crops, and the young sun
Has in the Ram his half course run,
And small fowls make melody
That sleep away all the night with open eye
(So nature pricks them and their spirit urges)
Then people long to go on pilgrimages
And palmers go to seek strange strands
To distant shrines, known in sundry lands,
And specially, from every shire's end
Of England, down to Canterbury they wend
The holy blissful martyr for to seek,
That gave them help before when they
   were sick.

The Year's Awakening

Thomas Hardy

How do you know that the pilgrim track
Along the belting zodiac
Swept by the sun in his seeming rounds
Is traced by now to the Fishes' bounds
And into the Ram, when weeks of cloud
Have wrapt the sky in a clammy shroud,
And never as yet a tint of spring
Has shown in the Earth's apparelling;
O vespering bird, how do you know,
How do you know?

How do you know, deep underground,
Hid in your bed from sight and sound,
Without a turn in temperature,
With weather life can scarce endure,
That light has won a fraction's strength,
And day put on some moments' length,
Whereof in merest rote will come,
Weeks hence, mild airs that do not numb;
O crocus root, how do you know,
How do you know?

Pippa's Song

Robert Browning

The year's at the spring,
And day's at the morn;
Morning's at seven;
The hill-side's dew-pearl'd;
The lark's on the wing;
The snail's on the thorn;
God's in His heaven –
All's right with the world!

Love's Labour's Lost

AN EXCERPT

William Shakespeare

When daisies pied and violets blue
And cuckoo-buds of yellow hue
And lady smocks all silver white
Do paint the meadows with delight,
The cuckoo then on every tree,
Mocks married men; for thus sings he;
Cuckoo.
Cuckoo, cuckoo! O word of fear,
Unpleasing to a married ear.

When shepherds pipe on oaten straws,
 And merry larks are ploughman's
clocks,
When turtles tread, and rooks and daws,
And maidens bleach their summer
    smocks,
The cuckoo then, on every tree,
Mocks married men, for thus sings he;
Cuckoo.
Cuckoo, cuckoo! O word of fear,
Unpleasing to a married ear.

April

Sara Teasdale

The roofs are shining from the rain.
The sparrows tritter as they fly,
And with a windy April grace
The little clouds go by.

Yet the back-yards are bare and brown
With only one unchanging tree –
I could not be so sure of Spring
Save that it sings in me.

I Bended Unto Me a Bough

T.E. Brown

I bended unto me a bough of May,
That I might see and smell:
It bore it in a sort of way,
It bore it very well.
But, when I let it backward sway,
Then it were hard to tell
With what a toss, with what a swing,
The dainty thing
Resumed its proper level,
And sent me to the devil.
I know it did – you doubt it?
I turned, and saw them whispering about it.

25

The Morning Land

Charles Mair

The light rains grandly from the distant wood,
For in the wood the hermit sun is hid;
So night draws back her curtains ebon-hued,
To close them round some eastern pyramid.

The listless dew lies shining on the grass,
And o'er the streams the light darts quick away,
And through the fields the morning sunbeams
   pass,
Shot from the opening portals of the day.

Still upward mounts the tireless eremite,
(While all the herald birds make loud acclaim)
Till o'er the woods he rounds upon our sight,
And, lo! the western world is all aflame.

From out the landscape lying 'neath the sun
The last sea-smelling, cloud-like mists arise;
The smoky woods grow clear, and, one by one,
The meadow blossoms ope their winking eyes.

Now pleased fancy starts with eager mien –
A-tiptoe, looking o'er the silent fields,
Where all the land is fresh and calm and green,
And every flow'r its balmy incense yields.

And I, who am upon no business bent,
A simple stroller through these dewy ways,
Feel that all things are with my future blent,
Yet see them in the light of by-gone days.

The Passionate Shepherd to His Love

Christopher Marlowe

Come live with me, and be my love,
And we will all the pleasures prove,
That Vallies, groves, hills and fields,
Woods, or steepie mountain yields.

And we will sit upon the Rocks,
Seeing the Shepherds feed their flocks,
By shallow Rivers, to whose falls,
Melodious birds sing Madrigals.

And I will make thee beds of Roses,
And a thousand fragrant posies,
A cap of flowers, and a kirtle,
Embroidered all with leaves of Myrtle.

A gown made of the finest wool,
Which from our pretty Lambs we pull,
Fair linèd slippers for the cold:
With buckles of the purest gold.

A belt of straw, and Ivy buds,
With Coral clasps and Amber studs,
And if these pleasures may thee move,
Come live with me, and be my Love.

The Shepherds Swains shall dance and sing,
For they delight each May-morning.
If these delights thy mind may move;
Then live with me, and be my Love.

Child's Song in Spring

Edith Nesbit

The silver birch is a dainty lady,
She wears a satin gown;
The elm tree makes the old churchyard shady,
She will not live in town.

The English oak is a sturdy fellow,
He gets his green coat late;
The willow is smart in a suit of yellow
While brown the beech trees wait.

Such a gay green gown God gives the larches –
As green as he is good!
The hazels hold up their arms for arches,
When spring rides through the wood.

The chestnut's proud, and the lilac's pretty,
The poplar's gentle and tall,
But the plane tree's kind to the poor dull city –
I love him best of all!

Loveliest of Trees

A.E. Housman

Loveliest of trees, the cherry now
Is hung with bloom along the bough,
And stands about the woodland ride
Wearing white for Eastertide.

Now, of my threescore years and ten,
Twenty will not come again,
And take from seventy springs a score,
It only leaves me fifty more.

And since to look at things in bloom
Fifty springs are little room,
About the woodlands I will go
To see the cherry hung with snow.

Boy Remembers the Field

Raymond Knister

What if the sun comes out
And the new furrows do not look smeared?

This is April, and the sumach candles
Have guttered long ago.
The crows in the twisted apple limbs
Are as moveless and dark.

Drops on the wires, cold cheeks,
The mist, the long snorts, silence…
The horses will steam when the sun comes;
Crows, go, shrieking.

Another bird now; sweet…
Pitiful life, useless,
Innocently creeping
On a useless planet
Again.

If any voice called, I would hear?
It has been the same before.
Soil glistens, the furrow rolls, sleet shifts,
brightens.

Spring

Gerard Manley Hopkins

Nothing is so beautiful as spring –
When weeds, in wheels, shoot long and
   lovely and lush;
Thrush's eggs look like little low
   heavens, and thrush
Through the echoing timber does so rinse
   and ring
The ear, it strikes like lightnings to hear
   him sing;
The glassy peartree leaves and blooms,
   they brush
The descending blue; that blue is all in a
   rush
With richness; the racing lambs too have
   fair their fling.

What is all this juice and all this joy?
A strain of the earth's sweet being in the
   beginning
In Eden garden. – Have, get, before it cloy,
Before it cloud, Christ, lord, and sour
   with sinning,
Innocent mind and Mayday in girl and boy,
Most, O maid's child, thy choice and
worthy the winning.

Spring Night

Sara Teasdale

The park is filled with night and fog,
The veils are drawn about the world,
The drowsy lights along the paths
Are dim and pearled.

Gold and gleaming the empty streets,
Gold and gleaming the misty lake,
The mirrored lights like sunken swords,
Glimmer and shake.

Oh, is it not enough to be
Here with this beauty over me?
My throat should ache with praise, and I
Should kneel in joy beneath the sky.
O, Beauty are you not enough?
Why am I crying after love,
With youth, a singing voice and eyes
To take earth's wonder with surprise?

Why have I put off my pride,
Why am I unsatisfied,–
I for whom the pensive night
Binds her cloudy hair with light,–
I, for whom all beauty burns
Like incense in a million urns?
O, Beauty, are you not enough?
Why am I crying after love?

Summer's Last Will and Testament

Thomas Nashe

Spring, the sweet spring, is the year's
   pleasant King,
When blooms each thing, then maids dance
   in a ring,
Cold doth not sting, the pretty birds do sing,
Cuckoo, jugge, jugge, pu we, to-witta-woo!

The Palm and May make country houses
   gay,
Lambs frisk and play, the Shepherds pipe all
   day,
And we hear aye birds tune this merry lay,
Cuckoo, jugge, jugge, pu we, to-witta-woo!

The fields breathe sweet, the daisies kiss our
   feet,
Young lovers meet, old wives a sunning sit;
In every street, these tunes our ears do greet,
Cuckoo, jugge, jugge, pu we, to-witta-woo!
Spring, the sweet spring.

The Echoing Green

William Blake

The sun does arise,
And make happy the skies;
The merry bells ring
To welcome the spring;
The skylark and thrush,
The birds of the bush,
Sing louder around
To the bell's cheerful sound,
While our sports shall be seen
On the Echoing Green.

Old John with white hair,
Does laugh away care,
Sitting under the oak,
Among the old folk.
They laugh at our play,
And soon they all say:
"Such, such were the joys
When we all, girls and boys,
In our youth time were seen
On the Echoing Green."

Till the little ones, weary,
No more can be merry;
The sun does descend,
And our sports have an end.
Round the laps of their mothers
Many sisters and brother,
Like birds in their nest,
Are ready for rest,
And sport no more seen
On the darkening Green.

The Spring

Thomas Carew

Now that winter's gone, the earth hath lost
Her snow-white robes, and now no more the frost
Candies the grass, or casts an icy cream
Upon the silver Lake, or Crystal stream:
But the warm Sun thaws the benumbèd Earth
And makes it tender, gives a sacred birth
To the dead Swallow; wakes in hollow tree
The drowsy Cuckoo, and the Humble-Bee.
Now do a choir of chirping Minstrels bring,
In triumph to the world, the youthful Spring.
The Valleys, hills, and woods, in rich array,
Welcome the coming of the long'd-for May,
Now all things smile; only my Love doth lour:
Nor hath the scalding Noon-day-Sun the power,
To melt that marble ice, which still doth hold
Her heart congeal'd, and makes her pity cold.
The Ox which lately did for shelter fly
Into the stall, doth now securely lie
In open fields; and love no more is made
By the fire side; but in the cooler shade
Amyntas now doth with his Cloris sleep
Under a Sycamore, and all things keep
Time with the season – only she doth carry
June in her eyes, in her heart January.

Spring Quiet

Christina Rossetti

Gone were but the Winter,
Come were but the Spring,
I would go to a covert
Where the birds sing;

Where in the whitethorn
Singeth a thrush,
And a robin sings
In the holly-bush.

Full of fresh scents
Are the budding boughs
Arching high over
A cool green house:

Full of sweet scents,
And whispering air
Which sayeth softly:
"We spread no snare;

"Here dwell in safety,
Here dwell alone,
With a clear stream
And a mossy stone.

"Here the sun shineth
Most shadily;
Here is heard an echo
Of the far sea,
Though far off it be."

Answer to a Child's Question

Samuel Taylor Coleridge

Do you ask what the birds say? The sparrows,
　the dove,
The linnet and thrush say, "I love and I love!"
In the winter they're silent – the wind is so strong;
What it says, I don't know, but it sings a loud song.
But green leaves, and blossoms, and sunny warm
　weather,
And singing, and loving – all come back together.
But the lark is so brimful of gladness and love,
The green fields below him, the blue sky above,
That he sings, and he sings; and for ever sings he –
"I love my Love, and my Love loves me!"

To Daffodils

Robert Herrick

Fair Daffodils, we weep to see
You haste away so soon;
As yet the early-rising sun
Has not attain'd his noon.
Stay, stay,
Until the hasting day
Has run
But to the even-song;
And, having pray'd together, we
Will go with you along.

We have short time to stay, as you,
We have as short a spring;
As quick a growth to meet decay,
As you, or anything.
We die
As your hours do, and dry
Away,
Like to the summer's rain;
Or as the pearls of morning's dew,
Ne'er to be found again.

A Bird Came Down the Walk

Emily Dickinson

A Bird came down the Walk –
He did not know I saw –
He bit an Angleworm in halves
And ate the fellow, raw,

And then he drank the Dew
From a convenient Grass –
And then hopped sideways to the Wall
To let a Beetle pass –

He glanced with rapid eyes
That hurried all around –
They looked like frightened Beads, I thought –
He stirred his Velvet Head

Like one in danger, Cautious,
I offered him a Crumb
And he unrolled his feathers
And rowed him softer home –

Than Oars divide the Ocean,
Too silver for a seam –
Or butterflies, off Banks of Noon
Leap, plashless as they swim.

A March Snow

Ella Wheeler Wilcox

Let the old snow be covered with the new:
The trampled snow, so soiled, and stained,
   and sodden.
Let it be hidden wholly from our view
By pure white flakes, all trackless and untrodden.
When Winter dies, low at the sweet Spring's feet
Let him be mantled in a clean, white sheet.

Let the old life be covered by the new:
The old past life so full of sad mistakes,
Let it be wholly hidden from the view
By deeds as white and silent as snow-flakes.

Ere this earth life melts in the eternal Spring
Let the white mantle of repentance fling
Soft drapery about it, fold on fold,
Even as the new snow covers up the old.

A Rainy Day in April

Francis Ledwidge

When the clouds shake their hyssops, and the
    rain
Like holy water falls upon the plain,
'Tis sweet to gaze upon the springing grain
And see your harvest born.

And sweet the little breeze of melody
The blackbird puffs upon the budding tree,
While the wild poppy lights upon the lea
And blazes 'mid the corn.

The skylark soars the freshening shower to hail,
And the meek daisy holds aloft her pail.
And Spring all radiant by the wayside pale
Sets up her rock and reel.

See how she weaves her mantle fold on fold,
Hemming the woods and carpeting the wold.
Her warp is of the green, her woof the gold,
The spinning world her wheel.

Daffodils

William Wordsworth

I wander'd lonely as a cloud
That floats on high o'er vales and hills,
When all at once I saw a crowd,
A host, of golden daffodils;
Beside the lake, beneath the trees,
Fluttering and dancing in the breeze.

Continuous as the stars that shine
And twinkle on the Milky Way,
They stretch'd in never-ending line
Along the margin of a bay:
Ten thousand saw I at a glance,
Tossing their heads in sprightly dance.

The waves besides them danced,
    but they
Out-did the sparkling waves in glee:
A poet could not but be gay,
In such a jocund company:
I gazed – and gazed – but little thought
What wealth the show to me had
    brought:

For oft, when on my couch I lie
In vacant or in pensive mood,
They flash upon that inward eye
Which is the bliss of solitude;
And then my heart with pleasure fills,
And dances with the daffodils.

To Spring

William Blake

O thou with dewy locks, who lookest down
Thro' the clear windows of the morning, turn
Thine angel eyes upon our western isle,
Which in full choir hails thy approach, O Spring!

The hills tell each other, and the listening
Valleys hear; all our longing eyes are turned
Up to thy bright pavilions: issue forth,
And let thy holy feet visit our clime.

Come o'er the eastern hills, and let our winds
Kiss thy perfumed garments; let us taste
Thy morn and evening breath; scatter thy pearls
Upon our love-sick land that mourns for thee.

O deck her forth with thy fair fingers; pour
Thy soft kisses on her bosom; and put
Thy golden crown upon her languished head,
Whose modest tresses were bound up for thee.

Lines Written in Early Spring

William Wordsworth

I heard a thousand blended notes,
While in a grove I sate reclined,
In that sweet mood when pleasant thoughts
Bring sad thoughts to the mind.

To her fair works did Nature link
The human soul that through me ran;
And much it grieved my heart to think
What man has made of man.

Through primrose tufts, in that green bower,
The periwinkle trailed its wreaths;
And 'tis my faith that every flower
Enjoys the air it breathes.

The birds around me hopped and played,
Their thoughts I cannot measure;–
But the least motion which they made,
It seemed a thrill of pleasure.

The budding twigs spread out their fan,
To catch the breezy air;
And I must think, do all I can,
That there was pleasure there.

If this belief from heaven be sent,
If such be Nature's holy plan,
Have I not reason to lament
What man has made of man?

Virtue

George Herbert

Sweet day, so cool, so calm, so bright,
The bridal of the earth and sky:
The dew shall weep thy fall to-night;
For thou must die.

Sweet rose, whose hue angry and brave
Bids the rash gazer wipe his eye:
The root is ever in its grave,
And thou must die.

Sweet spring, full of sweet days and roses,
A box where sweets compacted lie:
My music shows ye have your closes,
And all must die.

Only a sweet and virtuous soul,
Like seasoned timber, never gives;
But though the whole world turn to coal,
Then chiefly lives.

An April's Day

Henry Wadsworth Longfellow

When the warm sun, that brings
Seed-time and harvest, has returned again,
'Tis sweet to visit the still wood, where springs
The first flower of the plain.

I love the season well,
When forest glades are teeming with bright forms,
Nor dark and many-folded clouds foretell
The coming-on of storms.

From the earth's loosened mould
The sapling draws its sustenance, and thrives;
Though stricken to the heart with winter's cold,
The drooping tree revives.

The softly-warbled song
Comes from the pleasant woods, and colored
  wings
Glance quick in the bright sun, that moves along
The forest openings.

When the bright sunset fills
The silver woods with light, the green slope
  throws

Its shadows in the hollows of the hills,
And wide the upland glows.

And when the eve is born,
In the blue lake the sky, o'er-reaching far,
Is hollowed out and the moon dips her horn,
And twinkles many a star.

Inverted in the tide
Stand the gray rocks, and trembling shadows
    throw,
And the fair trees look over, side by side,
And see themselves below.

Sweet April! many a thought
Is wedded unto thee, as hearts are wed;
Nor shall they fail, till, to its autumn brought,
Life's golden fruit is shed.

Home Thoughts from Abroad

Robert Browning

Oh, to be in England
Now that April's there,
And whoever wakes in England
Sees, some morning, unaware,
That the lowest boughs and the brushwood sheaf
Round the elm-tree bole are in tiny leaf,
While the chaffinch sings on the orchard bough
In England – now!

And after April, when May follows,
And the whitethroat builds, and all the swallows –
Hark! where my blossomed pear-tree in the hedge
Leans to the field and scatters on the clover
Blossoms and dewdrops – at the bent spray's edge –
That's the wise thrush; he sings each song twice
    over,
Lest you should think he never could recapture
That first fine careless rapture!
And though the fields look rough with hoary dew,
All will be gay when noontide wakes anew
The buttercups, the little children's dower
 – Far brighter than this gaudy melon-flower!

In Springtime

Rudyard Kipling

My garden blazes brightly with the rose-bush
and the peach,
And the koil sings above it, in the siris by
the well,
From the creeper-covered trellis comes the
squirrel's chattering speech,
And the blue jay screams and flutters where
the cheery sat-bhai dwell.
But the rose has lost its fragrance, and the
koil's note is strange;
I am sick of endless sunshine, sick of blossom-
burdened bough.
Give me back the leafless woodlands where
the winds of Springtime range –
Give me back one day in England, for it's
Spring in England now!

Through the pines the gusts are booming,
o'er the brown fields blowing chill,
From the furrow of the ploughshare streams
the fragrance of the loam,

And the hawk nests on the cliffside and the
    jackdaw in the hill,
And my heart is back in England 'mid the
    sights and sounds of Home.
But the garland of the sacrifice this wealth of
    rose and peach is,
Ah! koil, little koil, singing on the siris bough,
In my ears the knell of exile your ceaseless
    bell like speech is –
Can you tell me aught of England or of
    Spring in England now?

...Summer days for me, When every leaf is on its tree;
When Robin's not a beggar, And Jenny Wren's a bride,
And larks hang singing, singing, singing,
Over the wheat-fields wide...

Summer

A Something in a Summer's Day

Emily Dickinson

A something in a summer's Day
As slow her flambeaux burn away
Which solemnizes me.

A something in a summer's noon—
A depth—an Azure—a perfume—
Transcending ecstasy.

And still within a summer's night
A something so transporting bright
I clap my hands to see—

Then veil my too inspecting face
Lest such a subtle—shimmering grace
Flutter too far for me—

The wizard fingers never rest—
The purple brook within the breast
Still chafes its narrow bed—

Still rears the East her amber Flag—
Guides still the sun along the Crag
His Caravan of Red—

So looking on—the night—the morn
Conclude the wonder gay—
And I meet, coming thro' the dews
Another summer's Day!

A Midsummer Night's Dream
AN EXCERPT

William Shakespeare

> I know a bank whereon the wild thyme blows,
> Where oxlips and the nodding violet grows
> Quite over-canopied with luscious woodbine,
> With sweet musk-roses, and with eglantine:
> There sleeps Titania some time of the night,
> Lull'd in these flowers with dances and delight;
> And there the snake throws her enamell'd skin,
> Weed wide enough to wrap a fairy in...

On the Grasshopper and the Cricket

John Keats

The poetry of earth is never dead:
When all the birds are faint with the hot sun,
And hide in cooling trees, a voice will run
From hedge to hedge about the new-mown mead;
That is the Grasshopper's – he takes the lead
In summer luxury, – he has never done
With his delights; for when tired out with fun
He rests at ease beneath some pleasant weed.
The poetry of earth is ceasing never:
On a lone winter evening, when the frost
Has wrought a silence, from the stove there shrills
The Cricket's song, in warmth increasing ever,
And seems to one in drowsiness half lost,
The Grasshopper's among some grassy hills.

Bed in Summer

Robert Louis Stevenson

In winter I get up at night
And dress by yellow candle-light.
In summer quite the other way,
I have to go to bed by day.

I have to go to bed and see
The birds still hopping on the tree,
Or hear the grown-up people's feet
Still going past me in the street.

And does it not seem hard to you,
When all the sky is clear and blue,
And I should like so much to play,
To have to go to bed by day?

The Garden

Andrew Marvell

What wond'rous Life in this I lead!
Ripe Apples drop about my head;
The Luscious Clusters of the Vine
Upon my Mouth do crush their Wine;
The Nectaren, and curious Peach,
Into my hands themselves do reach;
Stumbling on Melons, as I pass,
Insnar'd with Flow'rs, I fall on Grass.

Mean while the Mind, from pleasure
    less,
Withdraws into its happiness:
The Mind, that Ocean where each kind
Does streight its own resemblance find;
Yet it creates, transcending these,
Far other Worlds, and other Seas;
Annihilating all that's made
To a green Thought in a green Shade.

Here at the Fountains sliding foot,
Or at some Fruit-trees mossy root,
Casting the Bodies Vest aside,

My Soul into the boughs does glide:
There like a Bird it sits, and sings,
Then whets, and combs its silver Wings;
And, till prepar'd for longer flight,
 Waves in its Plumes the various Light.

To a Butterfly

William Wordsworth

I've watched you now a full half-hour,
Self-poised upon that yellow flower;
And, little Butterfly! indeed
I know not if you sleep or feed.
How motionless! – not frozen seas
More motionless! and then
What joy awaits you, when the breeze
Hath found you out among the trees,
And calls you forth again!

This plot of orchard-ground is ours;
My trees they are, my Sister's flowers;
Here rest your wing when they are weary;
Here lodge as in a sanctuary!
Come often to us, fear no wrong;
Sit near us on the bough!
We'll talk of sunshine and of song,
And summer days, when we were young;
Sweet childish days, that were as long
As twenty days are now.

Summer has Come Without the Rose

Arthur O'Shaughnessy

Has summer come without the rose,
Or left the bird behind?
Is the blue changed above thee,
O world! or am I blind?
Will you change every flower that grows,
Or only change this spot,
Where she who said, I love thee,
Now says, I love thee not?

The skies seemed true above thee,
The rose true on the tree;
The bird seemed true the summer through,
But all proved false to me.

An August Midnight

Thomas Hardy

I
A shaded lamp and a waving blind,
And the beat of a clock from a distant floor:
On this scene enter – winged, horned, and
    spined –
A longlegs, a moth, and a dumbledore;
While 'mid my page there idly stands
A sleepy fly, that rubs its hands…

II
Thus meet we five, in this still place,
At this point of time, at this point in space.
– My guests parade my new-penned ink,
Or bang at the lamp-glass, whirl, and sink.
"God's humblest, they!" I muse. Yet why?
They know Earth-secrets that know not I.

Recipe for a Salad

Sydney Smith

To make this condiment, your poet begs
The pounded yellow of two hard-boiled eggs;
Two boiled potatoes, passed through
   kitchen-sieve,
Smoothness and softness to the salad give;
Let onion atoms lurk within the bowl,
And, half-suspected, animate the whole.
Of mordant mustard add a single spoon,
Distrust the condiment that bites so soon;
But deem it not, thou man of herbs, a fault,
To add a double quantity of salt.
And, lastly, o'er the flavoured compound toss
A magic soup-spoon of anchovy sauce.
Oh green and glorious! Oh, herbaceous treat!
T'would tempt the dying anchorite to eat;
Back to the world he'd turn his fleeting soul,
And plunge his fingers in the salad bowl!
Serenely full, the epicure would say,
Fate can not harm me, I have dined today!

Moonlight, Summer Moonlight

Emily Brontë

'Tis moonlight, summer moonlight,
All soft and still and fair;
The solemn hour of midnight
Breathes sweet thoughts everywhere,

But most where trees are sending
Their breezy boughs on high,
Or stooping low are lending
A shelter from the sky.

And there in those wild bowers
A lovely form is laid;
Green grass and dew-steeped flowers
Wave gently round her head.

A Thunderstorm

Archibald Lampman

A moment the wild swallows like a flight
Of withered gust-caught leaves, serenely high,
Toss in the windrack up the muttering sky.
The leaves hang still. Above the weird twilight,
The hurrying centres of the storm unite
And spreading with huge trunk and rolling
   fringe,
Each wheeled upon its own tremendous hinge,
Tower darkening on. And now from heaven's
   height,
With the long roar of elm-trees swept and
   swayed,
And pelted waters, on the vanished plain
Plunges the blast. Behind the wild white flash
That splits abroad the pealing thunder-crash,
Over bleared fields and gardens disarrayed,
Column on column comes the drenching rain.

Heaven

Rupert Brooke

Fish (fly-replete, in depth of June,
Dawdling away their wat'ry noon)
Ponder deep wisdom, dark or clear,
Each secret fishy hope or fear.
Fish say, they have their Stream and
    Pond;
But is there anything Beyond?
This life cannot be All, they swear,
For how unpleasant, if it were!
One may not doubt that, somehow,
    Good
Shall come of Water and of Mud;
And, sure, the reverent eye must see
A Purpose in Liquidity.
We darkly know, by Faith we cry,
The future is not Wholly Dry.
Mud unto mud! – Death eddies near –
Not here the appointed End, not here!
But somewhere, beyond Space and
    Time,
Is wetter water, slimier slime!
And there (they trust) there swimmeth
    One

Who swam ere rivers were begun,
Immense, of fishy form and mind,
Squamous, omnipotent, and kind;
And under that Almighty Fin,
The littlest fish may enter in.
Oh! never fly conceals a hook,
Fish say, in the Eternal Brook,
But more than mundane weeds are there,
And mud, celestially fair;
Fat caterpillars drift around,
And Paradisal grubs are found;
Unfading moths, immortal flies,
And the worm that never dies.
And in that Heaven of all their wish,
There shall be no more land, say fish.

A Night-Rain in Summer

James Henry Leigh Hunt

Open the window, and let the air
Freshly blow upon face and hair,
And fill the room, as it fills the night,
With the breath of the rain's sweet might.
Hark! the burthen, swift and prone!
And how the odorous limes are blown!
Stormy Love's abroad, and keeps
Hopeful coil for gentle sleeps.

Not a blink shall burn to-night
In my chamber, of sordid light;
Nought will I have, not a window-pane,
'Twixt me and the air and the great good rain,
Which ever shall sing me sharp lullabies;
And God's own darkness shall close mine eyes;
And I will sleep, with all things blest,
In the pure earth-shadow of natural rest.

Paradise Lost
AN EXCERPT

John Milton

Now came still Evening on, and Twilight grey
Had in her sober livery all things clad;
Silence accompanied; for beast and bird,
They to their grassy couch, these to their nests
Were slunk, all but the wakeful nightingale;
She all night long her amorous descant sung:
Silence was pleased. Now glowed the
   firmament
With living sapphires; Hesperus, that led
The starry host, rode brightest, till the Moon,
Rising in clouded majesty, at length
Apparent queen, unveiled her peerless light,
And o'er the dark her silver mantle threw.

Adlestrop

Edward Thomas

Yes, I remember Adlestrop—
The name, because one afternoon
Of heat the express-train drew up there
Unwontedly. It was late June.

The steam hissed. Someone cleared his throat.
No one left and no one came
On the bare platform. What I saw
Was Adlestrop—only the name

And willows, willow-herb, and grass,
And meadowsweet, and haycocks dry,
No whit less still and lonely fair
Than the high cloudlets in the sky.

And for that minute a blackbird sang
Close by, and round him, mistier,
Farther and farther, all the birds
Of Oxfordshire and Gloucestershire.

Summer Shower

Emily Dickinson

> A drop fell on the apple tree,
> Another on the roof;
> A half a dozen kissed the eaves,
> And made the gables laugh.
>
> A few went out to help the brook,
> That went to help the sea.
> Myself conjectured, Were they pearls,
> What necklaces could be!
>
> The dust replaced in hoisted roads,
> The birds jocoser sung;
> The sunshine threw his hat away,
> The orchards spangles hung.
>
> The breezes brought dejected lutes,
> And bathed them in the glee;
> The East put out a single flag,
> And signed the fete away.

Love in Secret

John Clare

I met her in the greenest dells,
Where dewdrops pearl the wood bluebells;
The lost breeze kissed her bright blue eye,
The bee kissed and went singing by,
A sunbeam found a passage there,
A gold chain round her neck so fair;
As secret as the wild bee's song
She lay there all the summer long.

I hid my love in field and town
Till e'en the breeze would knock me down;
The bees seemed singing ballads o'er,
The fly's bass turned a lion's roar;
And even silence found a tongue
To haunt me all the summer long;
The riddle nature could not prove
Was nothing else but secret love.

Summer

Alexander Pope

See what delights in sylvan scenes appear!
Descending Gods have found Elysium here.
In woods bright Venus with Adonis stray'd,
And chaste Diana haunts the forest shade.
Come lovely nymph, and bless the silent hours,
When swains from shearing seek their nightly
   bow'rs;
When weary reapers quit the sultry field,
And crown'd with corn, their thanks to Ceres yield.
This harmless grove no lurking viper hides,
But in my breast the serpent Love abides.
Here bees from blossoms sip the rosy dew,
But your Alexis knows no sweets but you.
Oh deign to visit our forsaken seats,
The mossy fountains, and the green retreats!
Where-e'er you walk, cool gales shall fan the glade,
Trees, where you sit, shall crowd into a shade,
Where-e'er you tread, the blushing flow'rs shall rise,
And all things flourish where you turn your eyes.
Oh! How I long with you to pass my days,
Invoke the muses, and resound your praise;
Your praise the birds shall chant in ev'ry grove,
And winds shall waft it to the pow'rs above.
But wou'd you sing, and rival Orpheus' strain,

The wond'ring forests soon shou'd dance again,
The moving mountains hear the pow'rful call,
And headlong streams hang list'ning in their
    fall!
But see, the shepherds shun the noon-day heat,
The lowing herds to murm'ring brooks retreat,
To closer shades the panting flocks remove,
Ye Gods! And is there no relief for Love?
But soon the sun with milder rays descends
To the cool ocean, where his journey ends;
On me Love's fiercer flames for every prey,
By night he scorches, as he burns by day.

Standing Still

William Canton

Broad August burns in milky skies,
The world is blanched with hazy heat;
The vast green pasture, even, lies
Too hot and bright for eyes and feet.

Amid the grassy levels rears
The sycamore against the sun
The dark boughs of a hundred years
The emerald foliage of one.

Lulled in a dream of shade and sheen
With clement twilight thrown,
By that great cloud of floating green
A horse is standing, still as stone.

He stirs nor head nor hoof, although
The grass is fresh beneath the branch;
His tail alone swings to and fro
In graceful curves from haunch to haunch.

He stands quite lost, indifferent
To rock or pasture, trace or rein;
He feels the vaguely sweet content
Of perfect sloth in limb and brain.

Between the Dusk of a Summer Night

William Ernest Henley

Between the dusk of a summer night
And the dawn of a summer day,
We caught at a mood as it passed in flight,
And we bade it stoop and stay.
And what with the dawn of night began
With the dusk of day was done;
For that is the way of woman and man,
When a hazard has made them one.
Arc upon arc, from shade to shine,
The World went thundering free;
And what was his errand but hers and mine —
The lords of him, I and she?
O, it's die we must, but it's live we can,
And the marvel of earth and sun
Is all for the joy of woman and man
And the longing that makes them one.

A Calendar of Sonnets: June

Helen Hunt Jackson

O month whose promise and fulfilment blend,
And burst in one! it seems the earth can store
In all her roomy house no treasure more;
Of all her wealth no farthing have to spend
On fruit, when once this stintless flowering end.
And yet no tiniest flower shall fall before
It hath made ready at its hidden core
Its tithe of seed, which we may count and tend
Till harvest. Joy of blossomed love, for thee
Seems it no fairer thing can yet have birth?
No room is left for deeper ecstacy?
Watch well if seeds grow strong, to scatter free
Germs for thy future summers on the earth.
A joy which is but joy soon comes to dearth.

Pied Beauty

Gerard Manley Hopkins

Glory be to God for dappled things –
For skies of couple-colour as a brinded cow;
For rose-moles all in stipple upon trout that
    swim;
Fresh-firecoal chestnut-falls; finches' wings;
Landscape plotted and pieced – fold, fallow
    and plough;
And all trades, their gear and tackle and
    trim.

All things counter, original, spare, strange;
Whatever is fickle, freckled (who knows
    how?)
With swift, slow; sweet, sour; adazzle, dim;
He fathers-forth whose beauty is past
    change:
Praise him.

Summer Song

Ella Wheeler Wilcox

The meadow lark's trill and the brown thrush's
    whistle
From morning to evening fill all the sweet air,
And my heart is as light as the down of a thistle –
The world is so bright and the earth is so fair.
There is life in the wood, there is bloom on the
    meadow;
The air drops with songs that the merry birds sing.
The sunshine has won, in the battle with shadow,
And she's dressed the glad earth with robes of the
    spring.

The bee leaves his hive for the field of red clover
And the vale where the daisies bloom white as the
    snow,
And a mantle of warm yellow sunshine hangs over
The calm little pond, where the pale lilies grow.
In the woodland beyond it, a thousand gay voices
Are singing in chorus some jubilant air.
The bird and the bee and all nature rejoices,
The world is so bright, and the earth is so fair.

I am glad as a child, in this beautiful weather;
I have tossed all my burdens and trials away;
My heart is as light – yes, as light as a feather;–
I am care-free, and careless, and happy to-day.
Can it be there approaches a dark, dreary
to-morrow?
Can shadows e'er fall on this beautiful earth?
Ah! To-day is my own! No forebodings of
sorrow
Shall darken my skies, or shall dampen my
mirth.

Laughing Song

William Blake

When the green woods laugh with the voice of joy,
And the dimpling stream runs laughing by;
When the air does laugh with our merry wit,
And the green hill laughs with the noise of it;

When the meadows laugh with lively green,
And the grasshopper laughs in the merry scene,
When Mary and Susan and Emily
With their sweet round mouths sing 'Ha, ha he!'

When the painted birds laugh in the shade,
Where our table with cherries and nuts is spread:
Come live, and be merry, and join with me,
To sing the sweet chorus of 'Ha, ha, he!'

Dusk in June

Sara Teasdale

Evening, and all the birds
In a chorus of shimmering sound
Are easing their hearts of joy
For miles around.

The air is blue and sweet,
The few first stars are white,—
Oh let me like the birds
Sing before night.

Summer Night
AN EXCERPT FROM 'THE PRINCESS'

Alfred, Lord Tennyson

Now sleeps the crimson petal, now the white;
Nor waves the cypress in the palace walk;
Nor winks the gold fin in the porphyry font:
The fire-fly wakens: waken thou with me.

Now droops the milkwhite peacock like a ghost,
And like a ghost she glimmers on to me.

Now lies the Earth all Danaë to the stars,
And all thy heart lies open unto me.

Now slides the silent meteor on, and leaves
A shining furrow, as thy thoughts in me.

Now folds the lily all her sweetness up,
And slips into the bosom of the lake:
So fold thyself, my dearest, thou, and slip
Into my bosom and be lost in me.

Summer Sun

Robert Louis Stevenson

Great is the sun, and wide he goes
Through empty heaven with repose;
And in the blue and glowing days
More thick than rain he showers his rays.

Though closer still the blinds we pull
To keep the shady parlour cool,
Yet he will find a chink or two
To slip his golden fingers through.

The dusty attic spider-clad
He, through the keyhole, maketh glad;
And through the broken edge of tiles
Into the laddered hay-loft smiles.

Meantime his golden face around
He bares to all the garden ground,
And sheds a warm and glittering look
Among the ivy's inmost nook.

Above the hills, along the blue,
Round the bright air with footing true,
To please the child, to paint the rose,
The gardener of the World, he goes.

The Banks O'Doon

Robert Burns

Ye flowery banks o' bonie Doon,
How can ye blume sae fair;
How can ye chant, ye little birds,
And I sac fu' o' care!
Thou'll break my heart, thou bonie bird
That sings upon the bough;
Thou minds me o' the happy days
When my fause luve was true.

Thou'll break my heart, thou bonie bird
That sings beside thy matc;
For sae I sat, and sae I sang,
And wist na o' my fate.
Aft hae I rov'd by bonie Doon,
To see the woodbine twine,
And ilka bird sang o' its love,
And sae did I o' mine.

Wi' lightsome heart I pu'd a rose
Frae aff its thorny tree,
And my fause luver staw the rose,
But left the thorn wi' me.
Wi' lightsome heart I pu'd a rose,
Upon a morn in June:
And sae I flourish'd on the morn,
And sae was pu'd oor noon!

There Was a Boy

William Wordsworth

There was a Boy; ye knew him well, ye cliffs
And islands of Winander! – many a time,
At evening, when the earliest stars began
To move along the edges of the hills,
Rising or setting, would he stand alone,
Beneath the trees, or by the glimmering lake;
And there, with fingers interwoven, both hands
Pressed closely palm to palm and to his mouth
Uplifted, he, as through an instrument,
Blew mimic hootings to the silent owls,
That they might answer him. – And they would shout
Across the watery vale, and shout again,
Responsive to his call, – with quivering peals,
And long halloos, and screams, and echoes loud
Redoubled and redoubled; concourse wild
Of jocund din! And, when there came a pause
Of silence such as baffled his best skill:
Then, sometimes, in that silence, while he hung
Listening, a gentle shock of mild surprise
Has carried far into his heart the voice
Of mountain-torrents; or the visible scene
Would enter unawares into his mind
With all its solemn imagery, its rocks,
Its woods, and that uncertain heaven received
Into the bosom of the steady lake.

Ah! Sun-flower

William Blake

Ah, Sun-flower! weary of time,
Who countest the steps of the Sun,
Seeking after that sweet golden clime
Where the traveller's journey is done:

Where the Youth pined away with desire
And the pale Virgin shrouded in snow
Arise from their graves, and aspire
Where my Sun-flower wishes to go.

The Sun on the Bookcase

Thomas Hardy

Once more the cauldron of the sun
Smears the bookcase with winy red,
And here my page is, and there my bed,
And the apple-tree shadows travel along.
Soon their intangible track will be run,
And dusk grow strong
And they have fled.

Yes: now the boiling ball is gone,
And I have wasted another day…
But wasted—wasted, do I say?
Is it a waste to have imagined one
Beyond the hills there, who, anon,
My great deeds done,
Will be mine alway?

The Arbour

Anne Brontë

I'll rest me in this sheltered bower,
And look upon the clear blue sky
That smiles upon me through the trees,
Which stand so thickly clustering by;
And view their green and glossy leaves,
All glistening in the sunshine fair;
And list the rustling of their boughs,
So softly whispering through the air.

And while my ear drinks in the sound,
My winged soul shall fly away;
Reviewing long departed years
As one mild, beaming, autumn day;

And soaring on to future scenes,
Like hills and woods, and valleys green,
All basking in the summer's sun,
But distant still, and dimly seen.

Oh, list! 'tis summer's very breath
That gently shakes the rustling trees –
But look! the snow is on the ground –
How can I think of scenes like these?

'Tis but the frost that clears the air,
And gives the sky that lovely blue;
They're smiling in a winter's sun,
Those evergreens of sombre hue.

And winter's chill is on my heart –
How can I dream of future bliss?
How can my spirit soar away,
Confined by such a chain as this?

I Saw in Louisiana a Live-Oak Growing

Walt Whitman

I saw in Louisiana a live-oak growing,
All alone stood it and the moss hung down from
 the branches,
Without any companion it grew there uttering
  joyous leaves of dark green,
And its look, rude, unbending, lusty, made me
  think of myself,
But I wonder'd how it could utter joyous leaves
  standing alone there without its friend near,
  for I knew I could not,
And I broke off a twig with a certain number of
  leaves upon it, and twined around it a little
  moss,
And brought it away, and I have placed it in
  sight, in my room,
It is not needed to remind me as of my own dear
  friends,
(For I believe lately I think of little else than of
  them,)

Yet it remains to me a curious token, it makes
    me think of manly love;
And for all that, and though the live-oak glistens
    there in Louisiana solitary in a wide flat space,
Uttering joyous leaves all its life without a friend
    or lover near,
I know very well I could not.

Fair Summer Droops

Thomas Nashe

Fair summer droops, droop men and beasts
  therefore,
So fair a summer look for nevermore:
All good things vanish less than in a day,
Peace, plenty, pleasure, suddenly decay.
Go not yet away, bright soul of the sad year,
The earth is hell when thou leav'st to appear.

What, shall those flowers that decked thy
  garland erst,
Upon thy grave be wastefully dispersed?
O trees, consume your sap in sorrow's source,
Streams, turn to tears your tributary course.
Go not yet hence, bright soul of the sad year,
The earth is hell when thou leav'st to appear.

The Old Vicarage, Grantchester

Rupert Brooke

Just now the lilac is in bloom,
All before my little room;
And in my flower-beds, I think,
Smile the carnation and the pink;
And down the borders, well I know,
The poppy and the pansy blow…
Oh! There the chestnuts, summer through,
Beside the river make for you
A tunnel of green gloom, and sleep
Deeply above; and green and deep
The stream mysterious glides beneath,
Green as a dream and deep as death.
– Oh, damn! I know it! And I know
How the May fields all golden show,
And when the day is young and sweet,
Gild gloriously the bare feet
That run to bathe…
Du lieber Gott!

And after, ere the night is born,
Do hares come out about the corn?
Oh, is the water sweet and cool,
Gentle and brown, above the pool?
And laughs the immortal river still
Under the mill, under the mill?

Say, is there beauty yet to find?
And certainty? And Quiet kind?
Deep meadows yet, for to forget
The lies, and truths, and pain?…oh! yet
Stands the Church clock at ten to three?
And is there honey still for tea?

To Summer

William Blake

O thou who passest thro' our valleys in
Thy strength, curb thy fierce steeds, allay
   the heat
That flames from their large nostrils! thou, O
   Summer,
Oft pitched'st here thy goldent tent, and oft
Beneath our oaks hast slept, while we beheld
With joy thy ruddy limbs and flourishing hair.

Beneath our thickest shades we oft have heard
Thy voice, when noon upon his fervid car
Rode o'er the deep of heaven; beside our springs
Sit down, and in our mossy valleys, on
Some bank beside a river clear, throw thy
Silk draperies off, and rush into the stream:
Our valleys love the Summer in his pride.

Our bards are fam'd who strike the silver wire:
Our youth are bolder than the southern swains:
Our maidens fairer in the sprightly dance:
We lack not songs, nor instruments of joy,
Nor echoes sweet, nor waters clear as heaven,
Nor laurel wreaths against the sultry heat.

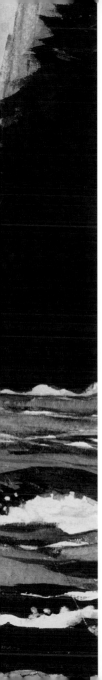

Good-Night to the Season

Winthrop Mackworth Praed

Good-night to the Season! 'tis over!
Gay dwellings no longer are gay;
The courtier, the gambler, the lover,
Are scatter'd like swallows away:
There's nobody left to invite one,
Except my good uncle and spouse;
My mistress is bathing in Brighton
My patron is sailing at Cowes:
For want of a better employment,
Till Ponto and Don can get out,
I'll cultivate rural enjoyment,
And angle immensely for trout…

Good-night to the Season! – the flowers
Of the grand horticultural fête,
When boudoirs were quitted for bowers,
And the fashion was not to be late;
When all who had money and leisure
Grew rural o'er ices and wines,
All pleasantly toiling for pleasure,
All hungrily pining for pines,
And making of beautiful speeches,
And marring of beautiful shows,
And feeding on delicate peaches,
And treading on delicate toes.

Good-night to the Season – another
Will come with its trifles and toys,
And hurry away, like its brother,
In sunshine, and odour, and noise.
Will it come with a rose or a briar?
Will it come with a blessing or curse?
Will its bonnets be lower or higher?
Will its morals be better or worse?
Will it find me grown thinner or fatter,
Or fonder of wrong or of right,
Or married, – or buried? – no matter,
Good-night to the Season, Good-night!

Summer

William Morris

Summer looked for long am I:
Much shall change or e'er I die.
Prithee take it not amiss
Though I weary thee with bliss.

...Come Sons of summer, by whose toil,
We are the Lords of Wine and Oil:
By whose tough labours, and rough hands,
We rip up first, then reap our lands...

Autumn

In Memoriam A.H.H.: XI

Alfred, Lord Tennyson

Calm is the morn without a sound,
Calm as to suit a calmer grief,
And only thro' the faded leaf
The chestnut pattering to the ground:
Calm and deep peace on this high wold,
And on these dews that drench the furze.
And all the silvery gossamers
That twinkle into green and gold:
Calm and still light on yon great plain
That sweeps with all its autumn bowers,
And crowded farms and lessening towers,
To mingle with the bounding main:

Calm and deep peace in this wide air,
These leaves that redden to the fall;
And in my heart, if calm at all,
If any calm, a calm despair:

Calm on the seas, and silver sleep,
And waves that sway themselves in rest,
And dead calm in that noble breast
Which heaves but with the heaving deep.

In September

Amy Levy

The sky is silver-grey; the long
Slow waves caress the shore.—
On such a day as this I have been glad,
Who shall be glad no more.

Poor Old Horse

Folk Song

My clothing was once of the linsey woolsey fine,
My tail it grew at length, my coat did likewise
   shine;
But now I'm growing old; my beauty does
   decay,
My master frowns upon me; one day I heard
   him say,

Poor old horse: poor old horse.

Once I was kept in the stable snug and warm,
To keep my tender limbs from any cold or harm;
But now in open fields, I am forced for to go,
In all sorts of weather, let it be hail, rain, freeze
   or snow.

Poor old horse: poor old horse.

Once I was fed on the very best corn and hay
That ever grew in yon fields, or in yon meadows
   gay;
But now there's no such doing can I find at all,
I'm glad to pick the green sprouts that grow
behind yon wall.

Poor old horse: poor old horse.

"You are old, you are cold, you are deaf, dull, dumb
   and slow,
You are not fit for anything, or in my team to draw.
You have eaten all my hay, you have spoiled all my
   straw,
So hang him, whip him, stick him, to the huntsman
   let him go."

Poor old horse: poor old horse.

My hide unto the tanners then I would freely give,
My body to the hound dogs, I would rather die than
   live,
Likewise my poor old bones that have carried you
   many a mile,
Over hedges, ditches, brooks, bridges, likewise gates
   and stiles.

Poor old horse: poor old horse.

Indian Summer

AN EXCERPT

Susanna Moodie

By the purple haze that lies
On the distant rocky heights,
By the deep blue of the skies,
By the smoky amber light,
Through the forest arches streaming
Where Nature on her throne sits dreaming,
And the sun is scarcely gleaming,
Through the cloudlets, snowy white, –
Winter's lovely herald greets us,
Ere the ice-crowned tyrant meets us.

This dreamy Indian-summer day,
Attunes the soul to tender sadness;
We love – but joy not in the ray –
It is not Summer's fervid gladness,
But a melancholy glory
Hovering softly round decay,
Like swan that sings her own sad story,
Ere she floats in death away.

Robin Redbreast

William Allingham

Good-bye, good-bye to Summer!
For Summer's nearly done;
The garden smiling faintly,
Cool breezes in the sun;
Our thrushes now are silent,
Our swallows flown away, –
But Robin's here, in coat of brown,
With ruddy breast-knot gay.
Robin, Robin Redbreast,
O Robin dear!
Robin singing sweetly
In the falling of the year.

Bright yellow, red, and orange,
The leaves come down in hosts;
The trees are Indian princes,
But soon they'll turn to ghosts;
The scanty pears and apples
Hang russet on the bough,
It's autumn, autumn, autumn late,
'Twill soon be Winter now.
Robin, Robin Redbreast,
O Robin dear!
And what will this poor Robin do?
For pinching times are near.

The fireside for the cricket,
The wheat-stack for the mouse,
When trembling night-winds whistle
And moan all round the house.
The frosty ways like iron,
The branches plumed with snow, —
Alas! in Winter, dead and dark,
Where can poor Robin go?
Robin, Robin Redbreast,
O Robin dear!
And a crumb of bread for Robin,
His little heart to cheer.

The Solitary Reaper

William Wordsworth

Behold her, single in the field,
Yon solitary Highland Lass!
Reaping and singing by herself;
Stop here, or gently pass!
Alone she cuts and binds the grain,
And sings a melancholy strain;
Oh listen! for the Vale profound
Is overflowing with the sound.

No Nightingales did ever chaunt
More welcome notes to weary bands
Of travellers in some shady haunt,
Among Arabian sands:
A voice so thrilling ne'er was heard
In springtime from the Cuckoo-bird,
Breaking the silence of the seas
Among the farthest Hebrides.

Will no one tell me what she sings? –
Perhaps the plaintive numbers flow
For old, unhappy, far-off things,
And battles long ago:
Or is it some more humble lay,
Familiar matter of today?
Some natural sorrow, loss, or pain,
That has been, and may be again?

Whate'er the theme, the Maiden sang
As if her song could have no ending;
I saw her singing at her work,
And o'er the sickle bending; –
I listened motionless and still;
And, as I mounted up the hill,
The music in my heart I bore,
Long after it was heard no more.

The Harvest of the Sea

John McCrae

The earth grows white with harvest; all day
   long
The sickles gleam, until the darkness weaves
Her web of silence o'er the thankful song
Of reapers bringing home the golden sheaves.

The wave tops whiten on the sea fields drear,
And men go forth at haggard dawn to reap;
But ever 'mid the gleaners' song we hear
The half-hushed sobbing of the hearts
   that weep.

Autumn Fires

Robert Louis Stevenson

In the other gardens
And all up the vale,
From the autumn bonfires
See the smoke trail!

Pleasant summer over
And all the summer flowers,
The red fire blazes,
The grey smoke towers.

Sing a song of seasons!
Something bright in all!
Flowers in the summer,
Fires in the fall!

Song in the Songless

George Meredith

They have no song, the sedges dry,
    And still they sing.
It is within my breast they sing,
    As I pass by.
Within my breast they touch a string,
    They wake a sigh.
There is but sound of sedges dry;
    In me they sing.

I am the Autumnal Sun

Henry David Thoreau

Sometimes a mortal feels in himself Nature
– not his Father but his Mother stirs
within him, and he becomes immortal with her
immortality. From time to time she claims
kindredship with us, and some globule
from her veins steals up into our own.

I am the autumnal sun,
With autumn gales my race is run;
When will the hazel put forth its flowers,
Or the grape ripen under my bowers?
When will the harvest or the hunter's moon
Turn my midnight into mid-noon?
I am all sere and yellow,
And to my core mellow.
The mast is dropping within my woods,
The winter is lurking within my moods,
And the rustling of the withered leaf
Is the constant music of my grief…

October

Francis Sherman

October's peace hath fallen on everything.
In the far west, above the pine-crowned hill,
With red and purple yet the heavens thrill—
The passing of the sun remembering.
A crow sails by on heavy, flapping wing,
(In some land, surely the young Spring hath
   her will!)
Below, the little city lieth still;
And on the river's breast the mist-wreaths
   cling.
Here, on this slope that yet hath known no
   plough,
The cattle wander homeward slowly now;
In shapeless clumps the ferns are brown and
   dead.
Among the fir-trees dusk is swiftly born;
The maples will be desolate by morn.
The last word of the summer hath been said.

Autumn

John Clare

The thistle down's flying, though the
winds are all still,
On the green grass now lying, now
mounting the hill,
The spring from the fountain now
boils like a pot;
Through stones past the counting, it
bubbles red-hot.

The ground parched and cracked is like
overbaked bread,
The greensward all wracked is bents
dried up and dead.
The fallow fields glitter like water
indeed,
And gossamers twitter, flung from
weed unto weed.

Hill-tops like hot iron glitter bright in
the sun,
And the rivers we're eyeing burn to
gold as they run;
Burning hot is the ground, liquid gold
is the air;
Whoever looks round sees Eternity
there.

An Autumn Rain-Scene

Thomas Hardy

There trudges one to a merry-making
With sturdy swing,
On whom the rain comes down.

To fetch the saving medicament
Is another bent,
On whom the rain comes down.

One slowly drives his herd to the stall
Ere ill befall,
On whom the rain comes down.

This bears his missives of life and death
With quickening breath,
On whom the rain comes down.

One watches for signals of wreck or war
From the hill afar,
On whom the rain comes down.

No care if he gain a shelter or none,
Unhired moves on,
On whom the rain comes down.

And another knows nought of its chilling fall
Upon him at all,
On whom the rain comes down.

To the Fringed Gentian

William Cullen Bryant

Thou blossom bright with autumn dew,
And colored with the heaven's own blue,
That openest when the quiet light
Succeeds the keen and frosty night.

Thou comest not when violets lean
O'er wandering brooks and springs unseen,
Or columbines, in purple dressed,
Nod o'er the ground-bird's hidden nest.

Thou waitest late and com'st alone,
When woods are bare and birds are flown,
And frosts and shortening days portend
The aged year is near his end.

Then doth thy sweet and quiet eye
Look through its fringes to the sky,
Blue—blue—as if that sky let fall
A flower from its cerulean wall.

I would that thus, when I shall see
The hour of death draw near to me,
Hope, blossoming within my heart,
May look to heaven as I depart.

Autumn: A Dirge

Percy Bysshe Shelley

The warm sun is falling, the bleak wind is wailing,
The bare boughs are sighing, the pale flowers are
    dying,
And the Year
On the earth is her death-bed, in a shroud of leaves
    dead,
Is lying.
Come, Months, come away,
From November to May,
In your saddest array;
Follow the bier
Of the dead cold Year,
And like dim shadows watch by her sepulchre.

The chill rain is falling, the nipped worm is
    crawling,
The rivers are swelling, the thunder is knelling
For the Year;
The blithe swallows are flown, and the lizards
    each gone
To his dwelling.

Come, Months, come away;
Put on white, black and gray;
Let your light sisters play—
Ye, follow the bier
Of the dead cold Year,
And make her grave green with tear on tear.

To Autumn

John Keats

Season of mists and mellow fruitfulness,
Close bosom-friend of the maturing sun;
Conspiring with him how to load and bless
With fruit the vines that round the
     thatch-eves run;
To bend with apples the moss'd
     cottage-trees,
And fill all fruit with ripeness to the core;
To swell the gourd, and plump the hazel
     shells
With a sweet kernel; to set budding more
And still more, later flowers for the bees,
Until they think warm days will never cease;
For Summer has o'er-brimm'd their clammy
     cells.

Who hath not seen Thee oft amid thy store?
Sometimes whoever seeks abroad may find
Thee sitting careless on a granary floor,
Thy hair soft-lifted by the winnowing wind;
Or on a half-reaped furrow sound asleep,
Drowsed with the fume of poppies, while
     thy hook

Spares the next swath and all its twined flowers;
And sometimes like a gleaner thou dost keep
Steady thy laden head across a brook;
Or by a cider-press, with patient look,
Thou watchest the last oozings, hours by hours.

Where are the songs of Spring? Aye, where are
    they?
Think not of them, – thou hast thy music too,
Whilst barred clouds bloom the soft-dying day
And touch the stubble-plains with rosy hue:
Then in a wailful choir the small gnats mourn
Among the river-sallows, borne aloft
Or sinking as the light wind lives or dies;
And full-grown lambs bleat from hilly bourn;
Hedge-crickets sing, and now with treble soft
The redbreast whistles from a garden-croft,
And gathering swallows twitter in the skies.

Indian Summer

Wilfred Campbell

Along the line of smoky hills
The crimson forest stands,
And all the day the blue-jay calls
Throughout the autumn lands.

Now by the brook the maple leans
With all his glory spread,
And all the sumachs on the hills
Have turned their green to red.

Now by great marshes wrapt in mist,
Or past some river's mouth,
Throughout the long, still autumn day
Wild birds are flying south.

Women's Harvest Song

Amy Lowell

I am waving a ripe sunflower,
I am scattering sunflower pollen to the four
    world-quarters.
I am joyful because of my melons,
I am joyful because of my beans,
I am joyful because of my squashes.

The sunflower waves.
So did the corn wave
When the wind blew against it,
So did my white corn bend
When the red lightning descended upon it,
It trembled as the sunflower
When the rain beat down its leaves.

Great is a ripe sunflower,
And great was the sun above my corn-fields.
His fingers lifted up the corn-ears,
His hands fashioned my melons,
And set my beans full in the pods.
Therefore my heart is happy

And I will lay many blue prayer-sticks at
    the shrine of Ta-wa.
I will give corn to Ta-wa,
Yellow corn, blue corn, black corn.
I wave the sunflower,
The sunflower heavy with pollen.
I wave it, I turn it, I sing,
Because I am happy.

A Song of Autumn

Adam Lindsay Gordon

'Where shall we go for our garlands glad
At the falling of the year,
When the burnt-up banks are yellow and sad,
When the boughs are yellow and sere?
Where are the old ones that once we had,
And when are the new ones near?
What shall we do for our garlands glad
At the falling of the year?'
'Child! can I tell where the garlands go?
Can I say where the lost leaves veer
On the brown-burnt banks, when the wild
  winds blow,
When they drift through the dead-wood drear?
Girl! when the garlands of next year glow,
You may gather again, my dear—
But I go where the last year's lost leaves go
At the falling of the year.'

Ruth

Thomas Hood

She stood breast-high amid the corn,
Clasp'd by the golden light of morn,
Like the sweetheart of the sun,
Who many a glowing kiss had won.

On her cheek an autumn flush,
Deeply ripen'd;—such a blush
In the midst of brown was born,
Like red poppies grown with corn.

Round her eyes her tresses fell,
Which were blackest none could tell,
But long lashes veil'd a light,
That had else been all too bright.

And her hat, with shady brim,
Made her tressy forehead dim;
Thus she stood amid the stooks,
Praising God with sweetest looks:—

Sure, I said, Heav'n did not mean,
Where I reap thou shouldst but glean,
Lay thy sheaf adown and come,
Share my harvest and my home.

November

Robert Bridges

The lonely season in lonely lands, when
fled
Are half the birds, and mists lie low,
and the sun
Is rarely seen, nor strayeth far from his
bed;
The short days pass unwelcomed one
by one.

Out by the ricks the mantled engine
stands
Crestfallen, deserted, – for now all
hands
Are told to the plough, – and ere it is
dawn appear
The teams following and crossing far
and near,
As hour by hour they broaden the
brown bands
Of the striped fields; and behind them
firk and prance
The heavy rooks, and daws grey-pated
dance:

As awhile, surmounting a crest, in sharp
    outline
(A miniature of toil, a gem's design,)
They are pictured, horses and men, or now
    near by
Above the lane they shout lifting the share,
By the trim hedgerow bloom'd with purple
    air;
Where, under the thorns, dead leaves in huddle lie
Packed by the gales of Autumn, and in and out
The small wrens glide
With a happy note of cheer,
And yellow amorets flutter above and about,
Gay, familiar in fear.

Autumn Within

Henry Wadsworth Longfellow

It is autumn; not without
But within me is the cold.
Youth and spring are all about;
It is I that have grown old.

Birds are darting through the air,
Singing, building without rest;
Life is stirring everywhere,
Save within my lonely breast.

There is silence: the dead leaves
Fall and rustle and are still;
Beats no flail upon the sheaves,
Comes no murmur from the mill.

Rugby Chapel: November 1857
AN EXCERPT

Matthew Arnold

Coldly, sadly descends
The autumn-evening. The field
Strewn with its dank yellow drifts
Of wither'd leaves, and the elms,
Fade into dimness apace,
Silent;— hardly a shout
From a few boys late at their play!
The lights come out in the street,
In the school-room windows;—but cold,
Solemn, unlighted, austere,
Through the gathering darkness, arise
The chapel-walls, in whose bound
Thou, my father! art laid.

There thou dost lie, in the gloom
Of the autumn evening. But ah!
That word, gloom, to my mind
Brings thee back, in the light
Of thy radiant vigour, again;
In the gloom of November we pass'd
Days not dark at thy side;
Seasons impair'd not the ray
Of thy buoyant cheerfulness clear.
Such thou wast! and I stand
In the autumn evening, and think
Of bygone autumns with thee.

Autumn Day

Rainer Maria Rilke

Lord: it is time. The summer was immense.
Lay your shadow on the sundials
and let loose the wind in the fields.

Bid the last fruits to be full;
give them another two more southerly days,
press them to ripeness, and chase
the last sweetness into the heavy wine.

Whoever has no house now will not build one
anymore.
Whoever is alone now will remain so for a long
time,
will stay up, read, write long letters,
and wander the avenues, up and down,
restlessly, while the leaves are blowing.

The Passing Day

William Ernest Henley

A late lark twitters from the quiet skies;
And from the west,
Where the sun, his day's work ended,
Lingers as in content,
There falls on the old, grey city
An influence luminous and serene,
A shining peace.

The smoke ascends
In a rosy-and-golden haze. The spires
Shine, and are changed. In the valley
Shadows rise. The lark sings on. The
    sun,
Closing his benediction,
Sinks, and the darkening air
Thrills with a sense of the triumphing
    night –
Night, with her train of stars
And her great gift of sleep.

So be my passing!
My task accomplished and the long day done,
My wages taken, and in my heart
Some late lark singing,
Let me be gathered to the quiet west,
The sundown splendid and serene,
Death.

Love in Autumn

Sara Teasdale

I sought among the drifting leaves,
The golden leaves that once were green,
To see if Love were hiding there
And peeping out between.

For thro' the silver showers of May
And thro' the summer's heavy heat,
In vain I sought his golden head
And light, fast-flying feet.

Perhaps when all the world is bare
And cruel winter holds the land,
The Love that finds no place to hide
Will run and catch my hand.

I shall not care to have him then,
I shall be bitter and a-cold—
It grows too late for frolicking
When all the world is old.

Then little hiding Love, come forth,
Come forth before the autumn goes,
And let us seek thro' ruined paths
The garden's last red rose.

To Autumn

William Blake

O Autumn, laden with fruit, and stainèd
With the blood of the grape, pass not, but sit
Beneath my shady roof; there thou may'st rest,
And tune thy jolly voice to my fresh pipe,
And all the daughters of the year shall dance!
Sing now the lusty song of fruits and flowers.

'The narrow bud opens her beauties to
The sun, and love runs in her thrilling veins;
Blossoms hang round the brows of Morning, and
Flourish down the bright cheek of modest Eve,
Till clust'ring Summer breaks forth into singing,
And feather'd clouds strew flowers round her
head.

'The spirits of the air live on the smells
Of fruit; and Joy, with pinions light, roves round
The gardens, or sits singing in the trees.'
Thus sang the jolly Autumn as he sat;
Then rose, girded himself, and o'er the bleak
Hills fled from our sight; but left his golden load.

The Last Rose of Summer

Charles Wolfe

That strain again? It seems to tell
Of something like a joy departed;
I love its mourning accents well,
Like voice of one, ah! broken-hearted.

That note that pensive dies away,
And can each answering thrill awaken,
It sadly, wildly, seems to say,
Thy meek heart mourns its truth forsaken.

Or there was one who never more
Shall meet thee with the looks of gladness,
When all of happier life was o'er,
When first began thy night of sadness.

Sweet mourner, cease that melting strain,
Too well it suits the grave's cold slumbers;
Too well the heart that loved in vain
Breathes, lives, and weeps in those wild
    numbers.

Ode to the West Wind

AN EXCERPT

Percy Bysshe Shelley

O wild West Wind, thou breath of Autumn's
being,
Thou, from whose unseen presence the
leaves dead
Are driven, like ghosts from an enchanter
fleeing,

Yellow, and black, and pale, and hectic red,
Pestilence-stricken multitudes: O thou,
Who chariotest to their dark wintry bed

The winged seeds, where they lie cold
and low,
Each like a corpse within its grave, until
Thine azure sister of the Spring shall blow

Her clarion o'er the dreaming earth, and fill
(Driving sweet buds like flocks to feed
in air)
With living hues and odours plain and hill:

Wild Spirit, which art moving everywhere;
Destroyer and preserver; hear, oh, hear!

The Autumn

Elizabeth Barrett Browning

Go, sit upon the lofty hill,
And turn your eyes around,
Where waving woods and waters wild
Do hymn an autumn sound.
The summer sun is faint on them—
The summer flowers depart—
Sit still—as all transform'd to stone,
Except your musing heart.

How there you sat in summer-time,
May yet be in your mind;
And how you heard the green woods sing
Beneath the freshening wind.
Though the same wind now blows around,
You would its blast recall;
For every breath that stirs the trees,
Doth cause a leaf to fall.

Oh! like that wind, is all the mirth
That flesh and dust impart:
We cannot bear its visitings,
When change is on the heart.
Gay words and jests may make us smile,
When Sorrow is asleep;

But other things must make us smile,
When Sorrow bids us weep!

The dearest hands that clasp our hands,—
Their presence may be o'er;
The dearest voice that meets our ear,
That tone may come no more!
Youth fades; and then, the joys of youth,
Which once refresh'd our mind,
Shall come—as, on those sighing woods,
The chilling autumn wind.

Hear not the wind—view not the woods;
Look out o'er vale and hill—
In spring, the sky encircled them—
The sky is round them still.
Come autumn's scathe—come winter's cold—
Come change—and human fate!
Whatever prospect Heaven doth bound,
Can ne'er be desolate.

October's Bright Blue Weather

Helen Hunt Jackson

O suns and skies and clouds of June,
And flowers of June together,
Ye cannot rival for one hour
October's bright blue weather;

When loud the bumble-bee makes haste,
Belated, thriftless vagrant,
And Golden-Rod is dying fast,
And lanes with grapes are fragrant;

When Gentians roll their fringes tight
To save them for the morning,
And chestnuts fall from satin burrs
Without a sound of warning;

When on the ground red apples lie
In piles like jewels shining,
And redder still on old stone walls
Are leaves of woodbine twining;

When all the lovely wayside things
Their white-winged seeds are sowing,
And in the fields, still green and fair,
Late aftermaths are growing;

When springs run low, and on the brooks,
In idle golden freighting,
Bright leaves sink noiseless in the hush
Of woods, for winter waiting;

When comrades seek sweet country haunts,
By twos and twos together,
And count like misers, hour by hour,
October's bright blue weather.

O suns and skies and flowers of June,
Count all your boasts together,
Love loveth best of all the year
October's bright blue weather.

... Now winter nights enlarge, The number of their hours;
And clouds their storms discharge, Upon the airy towers,
Let now the chimneys blaze, And cups o'erflow with wine,
Let well-tun'd words amaze, With harmony divine...

Winter

The Fall of the Leaf

Rosanna Leprohon

Ernest and sad the solemn tale
That the sighing winds give back,
Scatt'ring the leaves with mournful wail
O'er the forest's faded track;
Gay summer birds have left us now
For a warmer, brighter clime,
Where no leaden sky or leafless bough
Tell of change and winter-time.

Reapers have gathered golden store
Of maize and ripened grain,
And they'll seek the lonely fields no more
Till the springtide comes again.
But around the homestead's blazing hearth
Will they find sweet rest from toil,
And many an hour of harmless mirth
While the snow-storm piles the soil.

Then, why should we grieve for summer
   skies—
For its shady trees—its flowers,
Or the thousand light and pleasant ties
That endeared the sunny hours?
A few short months of snow and storm,
Of winter's chilling reign,
And summer, with smiles and glances warm,
Will gladden our earth again.

Plowman's Song

Raymond Knister

Turn under, plow,
My trouble;
Turn under griefs
And stubble.

Turn mouse's nest,
Gnawing years;
Old roots up
For new love's tears.

Turn, plow, the clods
For new thunder.
Turn under, plow,
Turn under.

Winter

Robert Southey

A wrinkled crabbed man they picture thee,
Old Winter, with a rugged beard as grey
As the long moss upon the apple-tree;
Blue-lipt, an icedrop at thy sharp blue nose,
Close muffled up, and on thy dreary way
Plodding alone through sleet and drifting
   snows.
They should have drawn thee by the high-heapt
   hearth,
Old Winter! seated in thy great armed chair,
Watching the children at their Christmas mirth;
Or circled by them as thy lips declare
Some merry jest, or tale of murder dire,
Or troubled spirit that disturbs the night,
Pausing at times to rouse the mouldering fire,
Or taste the old October brown and bright.

Winter's Song

AN EXCERPT FROM *LOVE'S LABOUR'S LOST*
William Shakespeare

When Icicles hang by the wall,
And Dick the Shepherd blows his nail;
And Tom bears Logs into the hall,
And Milk comes frozen home in pail:
When blood is nipt, and ways be foul
Then nightly sings the staring Owl
Tu-whit to-woo!
A merry note,
While greasy Joan doth keel the pot.

When all aloud the wind doth blow,
And coughing drowns the Parson's saw:
And birds sit brooding in the snow,
And Marian's nose looks red and raw:
When roasted Crabs hiss in the bowl,
When nightly sings the staring Owl,
Tu-whit to-woo!
A merry note,
While greasy Joan doth keel the pot.

The Winter Lakes

Wilfred Campbell

Out in a world of death far to the northward lying,
Under the sun and the moon, under the dusk and
the day;
Under the glimmer of stars and the purple of
sunsets dying,
Wan and waste and white, stretch the great lakes
away.

Never a bud of spring, never a laugh of summer,
Never a dream of love, never a song of bird;
But only the silence and white, the shores that
grow chiller and dumber,
Wherever the ice winds sob, and the griefs of
winter are heard.

Crags that are black and wet out of the grey lake
looming,
Under the sunset's flush and the pallid, faint
glimmer of dawn;
Shadowy, ghost-like shores, where midnight surfs
are booming
Thunders of wintry woe over the spaces wan.

Lands that loom like spectres, whited regions of
winter,

Wastes of desolate woods, deserts of water and
    shore;
A world of winter and death, within these
    regions who enter,
Lost to summer and life, go to return no more.

Moons that glimmer above, waters that lie white
    under,
Miles and miles of lake far out under the night;
Foaming crests of waves, surfs that shoreward
    thunder,
Shadowy shapes that flee, haunting the spaces
    white.

Lonely hidden bays, moon-lit, ice-rimmed,
    winding,
Fringed by forests and crags, haunted by
    shadowy shores;
Hushed from the outward strife, where the
    mighty surf is grinding
Death and hate on the rocks, as sandward and
    landward it roars.

Woods in Winter

Henry Wadsworth Longfellow

When winter winds are piercing chill,
And through the hawthorn blows the gale,
With solemn feet I tread the hill,
That overbrows the lonely vale.

O'er the bare upland, and away
Through the long reach of desert woods,
The embracing sunbeams chastely play,
And gladden these deep solitudes.

Where, twisted round the barren oak,
The summer vine in beauty clung,
And summer winds the stillness broke,
The crystal icicle is hung.

Where, from their frozen urns, mute springs
Pour out the river's gradual tide,
Shrilly the skater's iron rings,
And voices fill the woodland side.

Alas! how changed from the fair scene,
When birds sang out their mellow lay,
And winds were soft, and woods were green,
And the song ceased not with the day!

But still wild music is abroad,
Pale, desert woods! within your crowd;
And gathering winds, in hoarse accord,
Amid the vocal reeds pipe loud.

Chill airs and wintry winds! my ear
Has grown familiar with your song;
I hear it in the opening year,
I listen, and it cheers me long.

Winter Evening

An Excerpt from *The Task*

William Cowper

Now stir the fire, and close the shutters fast,
Let fall the curtains, wheel the sofa round,
And, while the bubbling and loud-hissing urn
Throws up a steamy column, and the cups,
That cheer but not inebriate, wait on each,
So let us welcome peaceful evening in…

Oh Winter, ruler of th'inverted year,…
I love thee, all unlovely as thou seemst,
And dreaded as thou art. Thou hold'st the sun
A prisoner in the yet undawning east,
Shortening his journey between morn and noon,
And hurrying him, impatient of his stay,
Down to the rosy west; but kindly still
Compensating his loss with the added hours
Of social converse and instructive ease,
And gathering, at short notice, in one group
The family dispersed, and fixing thought,
Not less dispersed by day-light and its cares.
I crown thee king of intimate delights,
Fire-side enjoyments, home-born happiness,
And all the comforts that the lowly roof
Of undisturbed retirement and the hours
Of long uninterrupted evening know.

Birds at Winter Nightfall

Thomas Hardy

Around the house the flakes fly faster,
And all the berries now are gone
From holly and cotoneaster
Around the house. The flakes fly!—faster
Shutting indoors that crumb-outcaster
We used to see upon the lawn
Around the house. The flakes fly faster,
And all the berries now are gone!

Emmonsail's Heath in Winter

John Clare

I love to see the old heath's withered brake
Mingle its crimpled leaves with furze and ling,
While the old heron from the lonely lake
Starts slow and flaps its melancholy wing,
An oddling crow in idle motion swing
On the half-rotten ash-tree's topmost twig,
Beside whose trunk the gypsy makes his bed.
Up flies the bouncing woodcock from the brig
Where a black quagmire quakes beneath the
    tread;
The fieldfares chatter in the whistling thorn
And for the haw round fields and closen rove,
And coy bumbarrels, twenty in a drove,
Flit down the hedgerows in the frozen plain
And hang on little twigs and start again.

On Ice

AN EXCERPT FROM *THE PRELUDE VOL. 1*
William Wordsworth

… All shod with steel
We hissed along the polished ice in games…
And not a voice was idle: with the din
Smitten, the precipices rang aloud;
The leafless trees and every icy crag
Tinkled like iron; while far distant hills
Into the tumult sent an alien sound
Of melancholy not unnoticed, while the
    stars
Eastward were sparkling clear, and in the
    west
The orange sky of evening died away.
Not seldom from the uproar I retired
Into a silent bay, or sportively
Glanced sideway, leaving the tumultuous
    throng,
To cut across the reflex of a star
That fled, and, flying still before me,
    gleamed
Upon the glassy plain: and oftentimes,
When we had given our bodies to the wind,
And all the shadowy banks on either side

Came sweeping through the darkness, spinning
   still
The rapid line of motion, then at once
Have I, reclining back upon my heels,
Stopped short; yet still the solitary cliffs
Wheeled by me – even as if the earth had rolled
With visible motion her diurnal round!
Behind me they did stretch in solemn train,
Feebler and feebler, and I stood and watched
Till all was tranquil as a dreamless sleep.

Snowflakes

Henry Wadsworth Longfellow

Out of the bosom of the Air,
Out of the cloud-folds of her garments shaken,
Over the woodlands brown and bare
Over the harvest-fields forsaken,
Silent and soft and slow
Descends the snow.

Even as our cloudy fancies take
Suddenly shape in some divine expression,
Even as the troubled heart doth make
In the white countenance confession
The troubled sky reveals
The grief it feels.

This is the poem of the air,
Slowly in silent syllables recorded;
This is the secret of despair,
Long in its cloudy bosom hoarded,
Now whispered and revealed
To wood and field.

A Winter Night

AN EXCERPT

Robert Burns

When biting Boreas, fell and dour,
Sharp shivers thro' the leafless bow'r;
When Phoebus gies a short-liv'd glow'r,
Far south the lift,
Dim-dark'ning thro' the flaky show'r,
Or whirling drift:

Ae night the storm the steeples rocked,
Poor Labour sweet in sleep was locked,
While burns, wi' snawy wreaths up-choked,
Wild-eddying swirl;
Or, thro' the mining outlet bocked,
Down headlong hurl:

List'ning the doors an' winnocks rattle,
I thought me on the ourie cattle,
Or silly sheep, wha bide this brattle
O' winter war,
And thro' the drift, deep-lairing, sprattle
Beneath a scar.

Ilk happing bird,—wee, helpless thing!
That, in the merry months o' spring,
Delighted me to hear thee sing,

What comes o' thee?
Whare wilt thou cow'r thy chittering wing,
An' close thy e'e?

Ev'n you, on murdering errands toil'd,
Lone from your savage homes exil'd,
The blood-stain'd roost, and sheep-cote spoil'd
My heart forgets,
While pityless the tempest wild
Sore on you beats!

Sonnet 97: How Like a Winter Hath My Absence Been

William Shakespeare

How like a winter hath my absence been
From thee, the pleasure of the fleeting year!
What freezings have I felt, what dark days seen!
What old December's bareness everywhere!
And yet this time removed was summer's time,
The teeming autumn, big with rich increase,
Bearing the wanton burden of the prime,
Like widowed wombs after their lords' decease:
Yet this abundant issue seemed to me
But hope of orphans, and unfathered fruit,
For summer and his pleasures wait on thee,
And thou away, the very birds are mute.
Or, if they sing, 'tis with so dull a cheer,
That leaves look pale, dreading the winter's near.

A January Morning

Archibald Lampman

The glittering roofs are still with frost; each
    worn
Black chimney builds into the quiet sky
Its curling pile to crumble silently.
Far out to westward on the edge of morn,
The slender misty city towers up-borne
Glimmer faint rose against the pallid blue;
And yonder on those northern hills, the hue
Of amethyst, hang fleeces dull as horn.
And here behind me come the woodmen's
    sleighs
With shouts and clamorous squeakings; might
    and main
Up the steep slope the horses stamp and strain,
Urged on by hoarse-tongued drivers cheeks
    ablaze,
Iced beards and frozen eyelids—team by team,
With frost-fringed flanks, and nostrils jetting
    steam.

December 13, 1836

AN EXCERPT

Emily Brontë

High waving heather, 'neath stormy blasts
  bending,
Midnight and moonlight and bright shining stars;
Darkness and glory rejoicingly blending,
Earth rising to heaven and heaven descending,
Man's spirit away from its drear dongeon
  sending,
Bursting the fetters and breaking the bars.

All down the mountain sides, wild forests
  lending
One mighty voice to the life-giving wind;
Rivers their banks in the jubilee rending,
Fast through the valleys a reckless course wending,
Wilder and deeper their waters extending,
Leaving a desolate desert behind.

Shining and lowering and swelling and dying,
Changing for ever from midnight to noon;
Roaring like thunder, like soft music sighing,
Shadows on shadows advancing and flying,
Lightning-bright flashes and deep gloom
  defying,
Coming as swiftly and fading as soon.

The Snow Storm

Ralph Waldo Emerson

Announced by all the trumpets of the sky,
Arrives the snow, and, driving o'er the fields,
Seems nowhere to alight: the whited air
Hides hill and woods, the river, and the heaven,
And veils the farmhouse at the garden's end.
The sled and traveller stopped, the courier's feet
Delayed, all friends shut out, the housemates sit
Around the radiant fireplace, enclosed
In a tumultuous privacy of storm.
Come see the north wind's masonry.
Out of an unseen quarry evermore
Furnished with tile, the fierce artificer
Curves his white bastions with projected roof
Round every windward stake, or tree, or door.
Speeding, the myriad-handed, his wild work
So fanciful, so savage, nought cares he
For number or proportion. Mockingly,
On coop or kennel he hangs Parian wreaths;
A swan-like form invests the hiddden thorn;
Fills up the famer's lane from wall to wall,
Maugre the farmer's sighs; and at the gate

A tapering turret overtops the work.
And when his hours are numbered, and
   the world
Is all his own, retiring, as he were not,
Leaves, when the sun appears, astonished Art
To mimic in slow structures, stone by stone,
Built in an age, the mad wind's night-work,
The frolic architecture of the snow.

The Darkling Thrush

Thomas Hardy

I leant upon a coppice gate
When Frost was spectre-gray,
And Winter's dregs made desolate
The weakening eye of day.
The tangled bine-stems scored the sky
Like strings of broken lyres,
And all mankind that haunted nigh
Had sought their household fires.

The land's sharp features seemed to be
The Century's corpse outleant,
His crypt the cloudy canopy,
The wind his death-lament.
The ancient pulse of germ and birth
Was shrunken hard and dry,
And every spirit upon earth
Seemed fervourless as I.

At once a voice arose among
The bleak twigs overhead
In a full-hearted evensong
Of joy illimited;
An aged thrush, frail, gaunt and small,
In blast-beruffled plume,

Had chosen thus to fling his soul
Upon the growing gloom.

So little cause for carolings
Of such ecstatic sound
Was written on terrestial things
Afar or nigh around,
That I could think there trembled through
His happy good-night air
Some blessed Hope, whereof he knew
And I was unaware.

December

Stuart Livingstone

The woods that summer loved are grey and
   bare;
The sombre trees stretch up their arms on high,
In mute appeal, against the leaden sky;
A flurry faint of snow is in the air.
All day the clouds have hung in heavy fold
Above the valley, where grey shadows steal;
And I, who sit and watch them, seem to feel
A touch of sadness as the day grows old.
But o'er my fancy comes a tender face,
A dream of curls that float like sunlight
   golden—
A subtle fragrance, filling all the place,
The whisper of a story that is olden—
Till breaks the sun through dull December skies,
And all the world is springtime in the deep blue
   of her eyes.

To Winter

William Blake

'O Winter! bar thine adamantine doors:
The north is thine; there hast thou built thy dark
Deep-founded habitation. Shake not thy roofs,
Nor bend thy pillars with thine iron car.'

He hears me not, but o'er the yawning deep
Rides heavy; his storms are unchain'd, sheathèd
In ribbèd steel; I dare not lift mine eyes,
For he hath rear'd his sceptre o'er the world.

Lo! now the direful monster, whose skin clings
To his strong bones, strides o'er the groaning rocks:
He withers all in silence, and in his hand
Unclothes the earth, and freezes up frail life.

He takes his seat upon the cliffs,— the mariner
Cries in vain. Poor little wretch, that deal'st
With storms!— till heaven smiles, and the monster
Is driv'n yelling to his caves beneath mount Hecla.

In Memorabilia Mortis

Francis Sherman

I marked the slow withdrawal of the year.
Out on the hills the scarlet maples shone—
The glad, first herald of triumphant dawn.
A robin's song fell through the silence – clear
As long ago it rang when June was here.
Then, suddenly, a few grey clouds were drawn
Across the sky; and all the song was gone,
And all the gold was quick to disappear.
That day the sun seemed loth to come again;
And all day long the low wind spoke of rain,
Far off, beyond the hills; and moaned, like one
Wounded, among the pines: as though the
  Earth,
Knowing some giant grief had come to birth,
Had wearied of the Summer and the Sun.

Winter Nightfall

Robert Bridges

The day begins to droop, –
Its course is done:
But nothing tells the place
Of the setting sun.

The hazy darkness deepens,
And up the lane
You may hear, but cannot see,
The homing wain.

The engine pants and hums
In the farm hard by:
Its lowering smoke is lost
In the lowering sky.

The soaking branches drip
And all night through
The dropping will not cease
In the avenue.

A tall man there in the house
Must keep his chair:
He knows he will never again
Breathe the spring air:

His heart is worn with work;
He is giddy and sick
If he rise to go as far
As the nearest rick:

He thinks of his morn of life,
His hale, strong years;
And braves as he may the night
Of darkness and tears.

February Twilight

Sara Teasdale

I stood beside a hill
Smooth with new-laid snow,
A single star looked out
From the cold evening glow.

There was no other creature
That saw what I could see—
I stood and watched the evening star
As long as it watched me.

Afternoon in February

Henry Wadsworth Longfellow

The day is ending,
The night is descending;
The marsh is frozen,
The river dead.

Through clouds like ashes
The red sun flashes
On village windows
That glimmer red.

The snow recommences;
The buried fences
Mark no longer
The road o'er the plain;

While through the meadows,
Like fearful shadows,
Slowly passes
A funeral train.

The bell is pealing,
And every feeling
Within me responds
To the dismal knell;

Shadows are trailing,
My heart is bewailing
And tolling within
Like a funeral bell.

To Flowers From Italy in Winter

Thomas Hardy

Sunned in the South, and here to-day;
—If all organic things
Be sentient, Flowers, as some men say,
What are your ponderings?

How can you stay, nor vanish quite
From this bleak spot of thorn,
And birch, and fir, and frozen white
Expanse of the forlorn?

Frail luckless exiles hither brought!
Your dust will not regain
Old sunny haunts of Classic thought
When you shall waste and wane;

But mix with alien earth, be lit
With frigid Boreal flame,
And not a sign remain in it
To tell men whence you came.

The Rainy Day

Henry Wadsworth Longfellow

The day is cold, and dark, and dreary;
It rains, and the wind is never weary;
The vine still clings to the moldering wall,
But at every gust the dead leaves fall,
And the day is dark and dreary.

My life is cold, and dark, and dreary;
It rains, and the wind is never weary;
My thoughts still cling to the moldering past,
But the hopes of youth fall thick in the blast
And the days are dark and dreary.

Be still, sad heart! and cease repining;
Behind the clouds is the sun still shining;
Thy fate is the common fate of all,
Into each life some rain must fall,
Some days must be dark and dreary.

The Falconer and his Hawk

Anon

The soaring hawk from fist that flies,
Her Falconer doth constrain
Sometime to range the ground unknown
To find her out again:
And if by sight or sound of bell,
His falcon he may see,
Wo ho ho, he cries with cheerful voice,
The gladdest man is he.

By lure then in finest sort,
He seeks to bring her in,
But if she full gorgéd be,
He can not so her win:
Although her becks and bending eyes,
She many proffers makes,
Wo ho ho, he cries, away she flies,
And so her leave she takes.

This woeful man with weary limbs
Runs wand'ring round about:
At length by noise of chattering pies,
His hawk again found out,

His heart was glad his eyes had seen
His falcon swift of flight:
Wo ho ho, he cries, she empty gorged,
Upon his lure doth light.

How glad was then the falconer there,
No pen nor tongue can tell:
He swam in bliss that lately felt
Like pains of cruel hell.
His hand sometime upon her train,
Sometime upon her breast
Wo ho ho, he cries with cheerful voice,
His heart was now at rest.

My dear, likewise behold thy love,
What pains he doth endure:
And now at length let pity move
To stoop unto his lure
A hood of silk and silver bells,
New gifts I promise thee:
Wo ho ho, I cry, I come then say,
Make me as glad as he.

Winter

William Morris

I am Winter, that do keep
Longing safe amidst of sleep:
Who shall say if I were dead
What should be remembered?

Winter Memories

David Henry Thoreau

Within the circuit of this plodding life
There enter moments of an azure hue,
Untarnished fair as is the violet
Or anemone, when the spring strew them
By some meandering rivulet, which make
The best philosophy untrue that aims
But to console man for his grievances.
I have remembered when the winter came,
High in my chamber in the frosty nights,
When in the still light of the cheerful moon,
On the every twig and rail and jutting spout,
The icy spears were adding to their length
Against the arrows of the coming sun,
How in the shimmering noon of winter past
Some unrecorded beam slanted across
The upland pastures where the Johnwort grew;
Or heard, amid the verdure of my mind,
The bee's long smothered hum, on the blue flag
Loitering amidst the mead; or busy rill,
Which now through all its course stands still and dumb

Its own memorial, – purling at its play
Along the slopes, and through the meadows
   next,
Until its youthful sound was hushed at last
In the staid current of the lowland stream;
Or seen the furrows shine but late upturned,
And where the fieldfare followed in the rear,
When all the fields around lay bound and hoar
Beneath a thick integument of snow.
So by God's cheap economy made rich
To go upon my winter's task again.

In Memoriam A. H. H.: XV

Alfred, Lord Tennyson

To-night the winds begin to rise
And roar from yonder dropping day:
The last red leaf is whirl'd away,
And rooks are blown about the skies;

The forest crack'd, the water curl'd,
The cattle huddled on the lea;
And wildly dash'd on tower and tree
The sunbeam strikes along the world:

And but for fancies, which aver
That all thy motions gently pass
Athwart a plane of molten glass,
I scarce could brook the strain and stir

That makes the barren branches loud;
And but for fear it is not so,
The wild unrest that lives in woe
Would dote and pore on yonder cloud

That rises upward always higher,
And onward drags a labouring breast,
And topples round the dreary west,
A looming bastion fringed with fire.

Blow, Blow, Thou Winter Wind

William Shakespeare

Blow, blow, thou winter wind
Thou art not so unkind
As man's ingratitude;
Thy tooth is not so keen,
Because thou art not seen,
Although thy breath be rude.

Heigh-ho! sing, heigh-ho! unto the green holly:
Most friendship is feigning, most loving mere
   folly:
Then heigh-ho, the holly!
This life is most jolly.

Freeze, freeze thou bitter sky,
That does not bite so nigh
As benefits forgot:
Though thou the waters warp,
Thy sting is not so sharp
As friend remembered not.
Heigh-ho! sing, heigh-ho! unto the green holly:
Most friendship is feigning, most loving mere
   folly:
Then heigh-ho, the holly!
This life is most jolly.

The Winter Galaxy

Charles Heavysege

The stars are glittering in the frosty sky,
Numerous as pebbles on a broad sea-coast;
And o'er the vault the cloud-like galaxy
Has marshalled its innumerable host.
Alive all heaven seems! with wondrous glow
Tenfold refulgent every star appears,
As if some wide, celestial gale did blow,
And thrice illume the ever-kindled spheres.
Orbs, with glad orbs rejoicing, burning, beam
Ray-crowned, with lambent lustre in their zones,
Till o'er the blue, bespangled spaces seem
Angels and great archangels on their thrones;
A host divine, whose eyes are sparkling gems,
And forms more bright than diamond diadems.

Winter Evening

Archibald Lampman

To-night the very horses springing by
Toss gold from whitened nostrils. In a dream
The streets that narrow to the westward gleam
Like rows of golden palaces; and high
From all the crowded chimneys tower and die
A thousand aureoles. Down in the west
The brimming plains beneath the sunset rest,
One burning sea of gold. Soon, soon shall fly
The glorious vision, and the hours shall feel
A mightier master; soon from height to height,
With silence and the sharp unpitying stars,
Stern creeping frosts, and winds that touch
  like steel,
Out of the depth beyond the eastern bars,
Glittering and still shall come the awful night.

The Quiet Snow

Raymond Knister

The quiet snow
Will splotch
Each in the row of cedars
With a fine
And patient hand;
Numb the harshness,
Tangle of that swamp.
It does not say, The sun
Does these things another way.

Even on hats of walkers,
The air of noise
And street-car ledges
It does not know
There should be hurry.

The Snowdrop

Anna Laetitia Barbauld

Already now the snowdrop dares appear,
The first pale blossom of th' unripen'd year;
As Flora's breath, by some transforming power,
Had chang'd an icicle into a flower,
Its name and hue the scentless plant retains,
And winter lingers in its icy veins.

Winter: My Secret

Christina Rossetti

I tell my secret? No indeed, not I:
Perhaps some day, who knows?
But not today; it froze, and blows, and snows,
And you're too curious: fie!
You want to hear it? well:
Only, my secret's mine, and I won't tell.

Or, after all, perhaps there's none:
Suppose there is no secret after all,
But only just my fun.
Today's a nipping day, a biting day;
In which one wants a shawl,
A veil, a cloak, and other wraps:
I cannot ope to every one who taps,
And let the draughts come whistling thro' my hall;
Come bounding and surrounding me,
Come buffeting, astounding me,
Nipping and clipping thro' my wraps and all.
I wear my mask for warmth: who ever shows
His nose to Russian snows
To be pecked at by every wind that blows?
You would not peck? I thank you for good will,
Believe, but leave that truth untested still.

Spring's an expansive time: yet I don't trust
March with its peck of dust,
Nor April with its rainbow-crowned brief
   showers,
Nor even May, whose flowers
One frost may wither thro' the sunless hours.
Perhaps some languid summer day,
When drowsy birds sing less and less,
And golden fruit is ripening to excess,
If there's not too much sun nor too much cloud,
And the warm wind is neither still nor loud,
Perhaps my secret I may say,
Or you may guess.

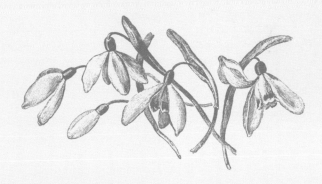

Biographical Notes

WILLIAM ALLINGHAM (c. 1824–1889) was born in Ballyshannon, Ireland. He worked as a customs officer in Ireland and England, during which time his first books were published, beginning with *Poems* (1850). After retirement he served as an editor at *Fraser's Magazine*.

MATTHEW ARNOLD (1822–1888) was born in Laleham, Middlesex, the son of schoolmaster and historian Thomas Arnold. His first volume of poetry, *The Strayed Reveller*, was published in 1849. Eight years later he was appointed Professor of Poetry at Oxford University.

ANNA LAETITIA BARBAULD (1743–1825) was born in Kibworth Harcourt, Leicestershire, the daughter of a Presbyterian minister. A poet, essayist and children's author, the success of Barbauld's writing career and political discourse was a significant breakthrough in the resistance of the gender roles of the era. Her poetry marked the foundations of English Romanticism.

WILLIAM BLAKE (1757–1827) was born into a middle-class family in London. A poet, painter and printmaker, he was educated by his mother and, later, at a drawing school and the Royal Academy. Blake is best remembered for his illuminated books, beginning with *All Religions Are One* (c. 1788).

ROBERT BRIDGES (1844–1930) was born in Walmer, Kent, and educated at Eton College and Corpus Christi College, Oxford. He studied medicine in London and practised as a doctor until, in 1882, lung disease forced him to retire. From that point, he devoted himself to writing and studying. In 1913, he became Poet Laureate, a title he held until his death.

ANNE BRONTË (1820–1849) was the youngest of six children who included the novelists Charlotte and Emily Brontë. As well as writing poems, Anne penned two novels, *Agnes Grey* (1847) and *The Tenant of Wildfell Hall* (1848), before falling ill with tuberculosis. She died, tragically, at the age of 29.

EMILY BRONTË (1818–1848) was born in Thornton, Yorkshire, the fifth of six children in the literary Brontë family. Her only volume of verse, *Poems of Currer, Ellis and Acton Bell* (1846), sold only two copies. She is best remembered for the novel *Wuthering Heights* (1847).

RUPERT BROOKE (1887–1915) was born at Rugby, Warwickshire. A graduate of Cambridge, his first collection of verse, *Poems*, was published in 1911. He died of blood poisoning while serving in the First World War.

T. E. BROWN (1830–1897) was born on the Isle of Man, the sixth of ten children. Educated at King William's College and, later, Christ Church, Oxford, he lived in England as a schoolmaster. His poetry, at once rugged and tender, tells of his island patriotism and simple piety.

ELIZABETH BARRETT BROWNING (1806–1861) was born Elizabeth Barrett Moulton-Barrett at Coixhoe Hall, near Durham, England. Her first book, *The Battle of Marathon*, a work of juvenilia, was published at the age of fourteen by her father. An accomplished and popular poet, she was thought of as a possible successor to William Wordsworth as England's Poet Laureate. She was married to the poet Robert Browning.

ROBERT BROWNING (1812–1889) was born in Camberwell, south London, the son of a well-paid clerk with the Bank of England. His education is said to have come primarily through his father's 6,000-volume library. Browning received little notice until the publication of his second volume of verse, *Paracelsus* (1835).

WILLIAM CULLEN BRYANT (1794–1878) was born in Cummington, Massachusetts. Educated at Williams College, he was admitted to the bar and worked for a time as a lawyer. He later relocated to New York City, where he worked as a journalist for *The New York Review* and *The New York Evening Post*. He used his position as editor of the latter publication in the fight against slavery.

ROBERT BURNS (1759–1796) was born in Alloway, South Ayrshire, Scotland, the son of a farming couple. His childhood was spent in poverty and much of his education came through his father who supplemented his modest income through tutoring. In 1783, he began composing poetry, employing the Ayrshire dialect. The publication three years later of his first volume of verse, *Poems, Chiefly in the Scottish Dialect*, established his reputation as national poet of Scotland.

WILFRED CAMPBELL (1858–1918) was born in Newmarket, Canada West (Ontario), the son of an Anglican minister. After an education received at a number of institutions, including the University of Toronto, University College, in 1884 Campbell was ordained into the Anglican priesthood. Seven years later, he suffered a crisis of faith, resigned from the church, and accepted a civil service position in Ottawa. He wrote six collections of verse and served as the editor of *The Oxford Book of Canadian Verse* (1913).

THOMAS CAMPION (1567–1620) was born in London. A poet, composer and physician, Campion studied at Cambridge. His earliest published poetry appears in Sir Philip Sidney's *Astrophel and Stella* (1591). Campion's early study of verse, *Observations in the Art of English Poesie* (1602), contains criticism of rhyming in poetry.

WILLIAM CANTON (1845–1926) was born in China to a Catholic family of civil servants. He studied for the priesthood before abandoning the vocation in favour of teaching and journalism. He wrote of science and religion in his poetry, but is now best known for his contributions to children's literature, including *The Invisible Playmate*, written for his daughter.

THOMAS CAREW (1595–1640), the son of Sir Thomas Carew, was born in West Wickham, Kent. Educated at Oxford, he served in a variety of diplomatic positions in Europe, before being appointed to the court of Charles I.

GEOFFREY CHAUCER (c.1343–1425) was born in London to a family of vintners. Although few details of his early life are documented, he went on to become an author, poet, diplomat and courtier in his lifetime. Known as 'the father of English literature', he is best remembered for the unfinished *Canterbury Tales*.

HUBERT CHURCH (1857–1932) was born in Hobart, Tasmania, educated in England and, from the age of 16, lived and worked in New Zealand. A novelist and poet, he is best known for his volumes of verse, *The West Wind* (1902) and *Poems* (1904).

JOHN CLARE (1793–1864) was born in Helpston, Cambridgeshire. The son of a farm labourer, his first verse was written in an attempt to prevent the eviction of his parents from their home. His highly praised first collection of verse, *Poems Descriptive of Rural Life and Scenery* (1820), led to his title 'the Northamptonshire Peasant Poet'.

SAMUEL TAYLOR COLERIDGE (1772–1834) was born in Ottery St Mary, Devonshire, the youngest of 16 children. He was educated at Jesus College and Cambridge. A poet, critic and philosopher, he was a key figure in the Romantic movement and counted Robert Southey and William Wordsworth among his closest friends. Coleridge's literary output was both aided and hindered by an addiction to opium.

WILLIAM COWPER (1731–1800) was born in Berkhamstead, Hertfordshire. After studying at Westminster School, his training for a career in law ended with the first of many bouts of mental illness. He sought strength through evangelical Christianity and, collaborating with John Newton, became one of the foremost composers of hymns.

EMILY DICKINSON (1832–1886) was born in Amherst, Massachusetts. Though one of the great American poets, only seven of her poems saw print during her lifetime – all anonymously. The first collection of her poetry, *Poems*, was published four years after her death.

RALPH WALDO EMERSON (1803–1882) was born in Boston. After attending Harvard, he worked as an educator, before returning to become a Unitarian minister like his father. After three years, in 1832, he resigned from the church. An essayist and poet, Emerson derived much of his income through his skills as a public orator.

ADAM LINDSAY GORDON (1833–1870) was born at Fayal in the Azores, the son of an English Army officer. Raised in Cheltenham,

England, he rejected the family tradition of military service, and, in 1853, emigrated to Australia. For a brief period he served in the South Australian mounted police, before taking up horse-breaking and racing. His first book of verse, *Ashtaroth, a Dramatic Lyric*, was published in 1867.

THOMAS HARDY (1840–1928) was born in Higher Bockhampton, Dorset, the son of a stonemason. Trained as an architect, in 1862 he moved to London where he was awarded prizes from the Royal Institute of British Architects and the Architectural Association. The author of several classic novels, including *Tess of the d'Ubervilles* (1891), *Far from the Madding Crowd* (1874) and *Jude the Obscure* (1895), Hardy turned his talents increasingly toward verse in later life.

CHARLES HEAVYSEGE (1816–1876) was probably born in Huddersfield, England. A woodcarver, he emigrated to Canada in 1853, and soon found work as a reporter for The Montreal Transcript and The Montreal Daily Witness. Heavysege asserted that there was some claim to nobility in his background. After his death, personal material was stolen from several different collections of his papers.

WILLIAM ERNEST HENLEY (1849–1902) was born in Gloucester, England, the son of a bookseller. As a child, he developed what was probably tubercular arthritis, a condition that interrupted his schooling and resulted in the amputation of part of his left leg. His earliest published poems were written while undergoing treatment at an Edinburgh hospital. After his recovery, Henley worked as an editor for *London* and *The Scots Observer*.

GEORGE HERBERT (1593–1633) was born in Montgomery, Wales. He studied at Trinity College, Cambridge, where he later taught, and served as a Member of Parliament. All of his surviving poems are religious in nature. His only collection, *The Temple: Sacred Poems and Private Ejaculations* (1633), was published posthumously.

ROBERT HERRICK (1591–1674) was born in London, the son of a wealthy goldsmith who committed suicide when the future poet was one year old. He attended Cambridge, took religious orders and became chaplain to the Duke of Buckingham.

THOMAS HOOD (1799–1845) was born in London, the son of a bookseller. He served in a number of editorial positions with *London Magazine*, *The Gem* and *The New Monthly Magazine*, and was a part-owner of the literary journal The Athenaeum.

GERARD MANLEY HOPKINS (1844–1889) was born in Stratford, Essex, the son of an insurance agent and amateur poet. During his studies at Oxford, he converted from Anglicanism to Roman Catholicism and eventually became a Jesuit priest. The first volume of Hopkins' verse was published nearly three decades after his death.

A. E. HOUSMAN (1859–1936) was born in Fockbury, Worcestershire. He was awarded a scholarship to Oxford, where he studied classics. For most of his life he taught Latin at Cambridge. Housman's masterpiece, *The Shropshire Lad* (1896), was rejected by several publishers and was eventually published at his own expense. His siblings, Laurence and Clemence Housman, were also writers.

JAMES HENRY LEIGH HUNT (1784–1859) was born in London to loyalist parents from Philadelphia. His first collection of poems, *Juvenalia*, was published in 1801. As a young man he embarked on a career as a critic, which involved his editorship of *The Examiner*, a newspaper founded by his brother, John Hunt.

HELEN HUNT JACKSON (1831–1885) was born Helen Maria Fiske in Amherst, Massachusetts. A writer of poetry, children's stories, novels and essays, her book, *Mercy Philbrick's Choice* (1876), is said to be a fictional portrait of her friend Emily Dickinson.

JOHN KEATS (1795–1821) was born in London. He was apprenticed to an apothecary-surgeon. His first volume of verse, *Poems*, published in 1817, was poorly received. Four years later, he died of tuberculosis while visiting Italy. He was soon recognized as one of the great poets of the English Romantic movement.

RUDYARD KIPLING (1865–1936) was born in Bombay (now Mumbai), India. He is best remembered for his books for children, *The Jungle Book* (1894), *The Second Jungle Book* (1895) and *Just So Stories* (1902). He wrote two collections of poetry, *Barrack-Room Ballads and Other Verses* (1893) and *Rudyard Kipling's Verse* (1923).

RAYMOND KNISTER (1899–1932) was born in Ruscom, Ontario. He studied at Victoria College, the University of Toronto and Iowa State University. Primarily a writer of poetry and short stories, only his first novel, *White Narcissus* (1929), was published during his lifetime. Knister drowned while swimming in Ontario's Lake St Clair.

ARCHIBALD LAMPMAN (1861–1899) was born in Morpeth, Canada West (Ontario). While studying at Trinity College, Toronto, he contributed his first poems to the literary magazine *Rouge et Noir*. After an unsuccessful attempt at teaching, he took a job with the Post Office in Ottawa. Two collections of verse, *Among the Millet and Other Poems* (1888) and *Lyrics of Earth* (1895) were published before his death.

FRANCIS LEDWIDGE (1887–1917) was born in County Meath, Ireland, the eighth of nine children in a poverty-striken family. A keen patriot and nationalist, he enlisted in the army at the outbreak of the First World War in 1914 and died during the Third Battle of Ypres in 1917. In his lifetime, his only published work was *Songs of the Field* (1915).

ROSANNA LEPROHON (1829–1879) was born Rosanna Eleanor Mullins in Montreal. Her first published poetry appeared in *The Literary Garland* at the age of 17. Primarily a writer of fiction, her best-known work is *Antoinette de Mirecourt* (1864).

AMY LEVY (1861–1899) was born in Clapham, London, to a Jewish family. Her writing career began early; her poem 'Ida Grey' appeared in print when she was just 14 years old. Her stories and poems, which touched on issues of feminism and Jewish identity, were published and praised by Oscar Wilde. Levy committed suicide at the age of 27.

STUART LIVINGSTONE was a Canadian. 'December', his only known poem, was published in *A Century of Canadian Sonnets* (1910), an anthology edited by Lawrence J. Burpee.

HENRY WADSWORTH LONGFELLOW (1807–1882) was born in Portland, Maine. Educated at Bowdoin College, he taught there and at Harvard. Among his more popular works are *Evangeline: A Tale of Acadie* (1847) and *The Song of Hiawatha* (1855).

AMY LOWELL (1874–1925) was born into a prominent Brookline, Massachusetts family in which the poet James Russell Lowell was her uncle and another poet, Robert Lowell, was her nephew. Mainly self-taught, from 1914 she lived with the actress Ada Dwyer Russell, the inspiration for many of her poems. She became a leading figure in the poetry movement known as 'Imagism' which led to her poetry moving closer to free verse.

CHARLES MAIR (1838–1927) was born in Lanark, Upper Canada (Ontario). He studied medicine at Queen's University, Canada but left to work in his family's lumber business. His first book, *Dreamland and Other Poems*, was published in 1868. He was a participant in the Red River Rebellion and was briefly imprisoned by the freedom fighter, Louis Riel. He is best remembered for the verse play *Tecumseh: A Drama* (1886).

KATHERINE MANSFIELD (1888–1923) was born Katherine Mansfield Beauchamp in Wellington, New Zealand. She studied at Queen's College, London, during which time she began to write sketches and prose poems. Although she returned to New Zealand, much of the rest of her life was spent moving around the literary circles of Europe. Her debut collection of verse, *Poems*, was published in 1923.

CHRISTOPHER MARLOWE (1564–1593) was most probably born in Canterbury, England. Marlowe was educated at Cambridge, during which time he wrote his first known drama, *Dido, Queen of Carthage* (1594), possibly in collaboration with Thomas Nashe. Considered the foremost Elizabethan playwright before William Shakespeare, he was murdered in mysterious circumstances.

ANDREW MARVELL (1621–1678) was born in Winestead-in-Holderness, East Yorkshire, the son of a clergyman. He attended Cambridge University and served many years as a Member of Parliament.

JOHN McCRAE (1872–1918) was born in Guelph, Ontario. He studied medicine at the University of Toronto and McGill. McCrae's earliest war poetry was written while serving in the Boer War. He died of pneumonia complicated by meningitis at a hospital in

BIOGRAPHICAL NOTES

Boulogne, France during the First World War. His only volume of poetry, *In Flanders Fields and Other Poems* (1919), was published posthumously.

GEORGE MEREDITH (1828–1909) was born in Portsmouth, England. He studied law, but ultimately chose to pursue a career in journalism. Although he is best remembered as a novelist, his first book was a collection of verse entitled *Poems* (1851). His first wife was the daughter of Thomas Love Peacock.

JOHN MILTON (1608–1674) was born in London, the son of a composer. He studied at Cambridge, during which time he wrote some of his finest poetry. His masterpiece, *Paradise Lost*, was published in 1667.

SUSANNA MOODIE (1803–1885) was born Susanna Strickland in Bungay, England. The younger sister of Catharine Parr Traill, she was one of a family of writers. Her first book, *Spartacus*, was published in 1822. In 1832, she relocated with her husband and daughter, emigrating to Upper Canada. Her early pioneer experiences are recorded in her best-known work, *Roughing It in the Bush* (1852).

WILLIAM MORRIS (1834–1896) was born in Walthamstow, England. He was educated at Oxford, where he became friends with Edward Burne-Jones and Dante Gabriel Rossetti. Although he is remembered today for his designs in furniture, decoration and architecture, Morris was also a prolific writer. His first book of verse, *The Defence of Guenevere and Other Poems*, was published in 1858.

THOMAS NASHE (1567–?1601) was probably born in Lowestoft, Suffolk. He began studies at Cambridge, but left for an unknown reason. By 1589, he was living in London, where he pursued a life in letters as a poet, playwright, pamphleteer and satirist. Although he is memorialized in Charles Fitzjeoffry's *Affaniae* (1601), his death is otherwise unrecorded.

EDITH NESBIT (1858–1924) was born in London. A writer of poetry, novels and short stories, she received commercial and critical success for her children's novels, including *The Railway Children* (1906).

244

ARTHUR O'SHAUGHNESSY (1844–1881) was born in London. Employed from a young age at the British Museum, his true interests lay in literature. O'Shaughnessy's first collection of verse, *Epic of Women*, was published in 1870.

ALEXANDER POPE (1688–1744) was born in London. His first published verse appeared in *Poetical Miscellanies* (1709), an anthology published by Jacob Tonson. His most famous poem, 'The Rape of the Lock', was published in 1712.

WINTHROP MACKWORTH PRAED (1802–1839) was born in London. An eminent politician as well as a poet, his verse was characterized by humorous satire, vivacity and wit. At his former college, Eton, his name lives on today in the form of the Praed society, the school's exclusive poetry society.

RAINER MARIA RILKE (1875–1926) was born in Prague and is generally considered to be one of the German language's greatest poets of the 20th century. His first collection of poetry, *Leben und Leiber* (*Life and Songs*) was published in 1894.

CHRISTINA GEORGINA ROSSETTI (1830–1894) was born into a literary household in London. Her siblings included Dante Gabriel Rossetti, Michael Rossetti and Maria Francesca Rossetti. Her first collection of verse, *Goblin Market and Other Poems*, was published in 1862.

WILLIAM SHAKESPEARE (1564–1616) was born in England at Stratford-on-Avon. A poet and playwright, he is widely considered the greatest writer in the English language.

PERCY BYSSHE SHELLEY (1792–1822), the son of Sir Timothy Shelley, was raised in Sussex, England. A graduate of Eton, he enrolled at Oxford in 1810, only to be expelled the following year as the author of the pamphlet, *The Necessity of Atheism* (1811). His first published poetry was *Queen Mab* (1813). Shelley drowned the month before his 30th birthday. His second wife was Mary Shelley.

FRANCIS SHERMAN (1871–1926) was born in Fredericton, New Brunswick. He studied at the University of New Brunswick, but his poor financial situation forced him to leave. He began what would become an extremely successful career in banking. Sherman's first collection of poems, *Matins*, was published in 1896. Although other volumes followed, within five years he had ceased writing verse.

SYDNEY SMITH (1771–1845) was born in Essex, England, the son of a merchant. He became an Anglican clergyman and celebrated preacher. His *Recipe for a Salad* lived on long after his death amongst keen homemakers in the United States.

ROBERT SOUTHEY (1774–1843) was born in Bristol, England. Educated at Oxford, he was a literary scholar and biographer. In 1813, he was made Poet Laureate, a position offered to him after Sir Walter Scott refused it.

ROBERT LOUIS STEVENSON (1850–1894) was born in Edinburgh. He studied law at the University of Edinburgh, though he never practised. He travelled widely and wrote some of the greatest classics of the Victorian era, including *Treasure Island* (1883), *The Strange Case of Dr Jekyll and Mr Hyde* (1886) and *Kidnapped* (1886).

SARA TEASDALE (1884–1933) was born in St Louis, Missouri. A sickly child, until the age of nine she was unable to attend school. Her first volume of verse, *Helen of Troy and Other Poems*, was published in 1911. Teasdale committed suicide at the age of 48.

ALFRED, LORD TENNYSON (1809–1892) was born in Somersby, Lincolnshire, the son of a clergyman. He was educated at Cambridge, during which time his first book, *Poems, Chiefly Lyrical* (1830), was published. He was forced to abandon his studies following the death of his father. In 1850, he was appointed Poet Laureate, a position he held for over four decades.

EDWARD THOMAS (1878–1917) was born in London. After studying at Oxford, he began a life in letters as an author, editor and critic. He did not begin writing verse until 1914, the year before he joined up for the First World War. He was killed by a shell at Arras, France.

HENRY DAVID THOREAU (1817–1862) was born in Concord, Massachusetts. Educated at Harvard, he is best known for the essay

Civil Disobedience (1849) and the novel *Walden* (1854), his reflection upon simple living.

WALT WHITMAN (1819–1892) was born in West Hills, New York. After leaving school he undertook a variety of occupations, including printer, carpenter, teacher and newspaper editor. Whitman's key work, *Leaves of Grass*, was first published in 1855 as a slim volume containing 12 long poems. He spent much of the remainder of his life revising the work, adding and, on occasion, removing verse. The last edition, published the year before his death, featured nearly 400 poems.

ELLA WHEELER WILCOX (1850–1919) was born in Jonestown, Wisconsin. An extremely prolific and popular poet, she wrote dozens of volumes of poetry.

CHARLES WOLFE (1791–1823) was born in Blackhall, Ireland. He studied at Trinity College, Dublin and was ordained as a minister in the Church of Ireland. His only volume of verse, *Poetical Remains*, appeared two years after his death from tuberculosis.

WILLIAM WORDSWORTH (1770–1850) was born in Cockermouth on the River Derwent, England. He graduated from Cambridge in 1791 and two years later published his first two collections of verse, *An Evening Walk* and *Descriptive Sketches*. In 1843, he was made Poet Laureate, a position he held until his death. His sister was the poet and diarist Dorothy Wordsworth.

Index of Poets

Allingham, William.............. 136

Anonymous 132, 220

Arnold, Matthew.................. 162

Barbauld, Anna Laetitia 232

Blake, William 12, 40, 55, 104, 112, 123, 169, 210

Bridges, Robert 160

Brontë, Anne.......................... 114

Brontë, Emily 82

Brooke, Rupert..................... 84, 121

Brown, T.E. 25

Browning, Elizabeth Barrett.................................. 174

Browning, Robert 21, 63

Bryant, William Cullen 150

Burns, Robert 109, 198

Campbell, Wilfred 155, 186

Campion, Thomas 179

Canton, William.................... 96

Carew, Thomas 43

Chaucer, Geoffrey 19

Church, Hubert 11

Clare, John 14, 93, 147, 193

Coleridge, Samuel Taylor 46

Cowper, William 190

Dickinson, Emily 10, 49, 68, 91

Emerson, Ralph Waldon...... 204

Gordon, Adam Lindsay 158

Hardy, Thomas 20, 79, 113, 148, 192, 207, 218

Heavysege, Charles.............. 229

Henley, William Ernest........ 98, 167

Herbert, George 59

Herrick, Robert 9, 47, 129

Hood, Thomas 159

Hopkins, Gerard Manley 35, 101

Housman, A.E. 32

Hunt, James Henry Leigh .. 87

Hunt Jackson, Helen 99, 170

Keats, John 72, 152

Kipling, Rudyard.................. 64

Knister, Raymond 33, 182, 231

Lampman, Archibald 83, 201, 230

Ledwidge, Francis................ 51

Leprohon, Rosanna 180

Levy, Amy.............................. 165

Livingstone, Stuart 209

Longfellow, Henry Wadsworth........................... 60, 177, 188, 197, 216, 219

Lowell, Amy.......................... 13, 156

Mair, Charles 26

Mansfield, Katherine 16

Marlowe, Christopher 29

Marvell, Andrew 75

McCrae, John 141

Meredith, George.................. 143

Milton, John 89

Moodie, Susanna 135

Morris, William 127, 223

Nashe, Thomas 39, 119

Nesbit, Edith 31

O'Shaughnessy, Arthur........ 78

Pope, Alexander 94

Praed, Winthrop Mackworth........................... 125

Rilke, Rainer Maria 164

Rossetti, Christina 44, 67, 234

Shakespeare, William 22, 71, 185, 200, 228

Shelley, Percy Bysshe 151, 172

Sherman, Francis 145, 211

Smith, Sydney 81

Southey, Robert 183

Stevenson, Robert Louis...... 73, 142

Teasdale, Sara........................ 24, 36, 105, 168, 215

Tennyson, Lord Alfred 106, 130, 227

Thomas, Edward 90

Thoreau, Henry David 144, 224

Whitman, Walt...................... 117

Wilcox, Ella Wheeler 50, 102

Wolfe, Charles 176

Wordsworth, William 52, 56, 77, 111, 194

Index of Titles

Adlestrop 90

Afternoon in February 216

Ah! Sun-flower 112

An April's Day 60

An August Midnight 79

An Autumn Rain-Scene........ 148

Answer to a Child's
  Question 46

April 24

Arbour, The 114

Autumn 147,
  174

Autumn Day 164

Autumn Fires 142

Autumn Within...................... 177

Autumn: A Dirge 151

Banks o' Doon, The 109

Bed in Summer 73

Between the Dusk of a Summer
  Night 98

Bird Came Down the
  Walk, A 49

Birds at Winter Nightfall 192

Blossom, The 12

Blow, Blow, Thou Winter
  Wind...................................... 228

Boy Remembers the Field 33

Calendar of Sonnets:
  June, A 99

Child's Song in Spring.......... 31

Daffodils 52

Darkling Thrush, The............ 207

December................................ 209

December 13, 1836 202

Dusk in June 105

Echoing Green, The 40

Emmonsail's Heath in
  Winter 193

Fair Summer Droops 119

Falconer and his Hawk, The.. 220

Fall of the Leaf, The 180

February Twilight.................. 215

Garden, The............................ 75

Good-Night to the Season.... 125

Harvest of the Sea, The 141

Heaven.................................... 84

Home Thoughts from
  Abroad.................................. 63

I am the Autumnal Sun 144

I Bended Unto Me a Bough
  of May 25

I Saw in Louisanna a
  Live-Oak Growing.............. 117

In Memorabilia Mortis.......... 211

In Memoriam A.H.H.: XI...... 130

In Memoriam A.H.H.: XV 227

In September 165

In Springtime 64

Indian Summer 135,
  155

January Morning, A 201

Last Rose of Summer, The.... 176

Laughing Song 104

Light Exists in Spring, A 10

Lines Written in Early
  Spring 56

Love in Autumn 168
Love in Secret 93
Love's Labour's Lost 22
Loveliest of Trees 32
March Snow, A 50
Midsummer Night's
    Dream, A 71
Moonlight, Summer
    Moonlight 82
Morning Land, The 26
Night-Rain in Summer, A 87
November 160
October 145
October's Bright Blue
    Weather 170
Ode to the West
    Wind 172
Old Vicarage, Grantchester,
    The 121
On Ice 194
On the Grasshopper and the
    Cricket 72
Paradise Lost 89
Passionate Shepherd to his
    Love, The 29
Passing Day, The 167
Pied Beauty 101
Pippa's Song 21
Plowman's Song 182
Poor Old Horse 132
Prologue to the Canterbury
    Tales 19
Quiet Snow, The 231
Rainy Day, The 219
Rainy Day in April, A 51
Recipe for a Salad 81

Robin Redbreast 136
Rugby Chapel:
    November 1857 162
Ruth 159
Snow Storm, The 204
Snowdrop, The 232
Snowflakes 197
Solitary Reaper, The 139
Something in a Summer's
    Day, A 68
Song in the Songless 143
Song of Autumn, A 158
Sonnet 97: How Like a Winter
    Hath My Absence Been 200
Sonnet: The Crow 14
Spring 35
Spring in New Zealand 11
Spring Night 36
Spring Quiet 44
Spring Wind in London 16
Spring, The 43
Standing Still 96
Summer 94,
    127
Summer has Come Without
    the Rose 78
Summer Night 106
Summer Shower 91
Summer Song 102
Summer Sun 108
Summer's Last Will and
    Testament 39
Sun on the Bookcase, The 113
There was a Boy 111
Thunderstorm, A 83
To a Butterfly 77

To an Early Daffodil 13

To Autumn 152, 169

To Daffodils 47

To Flowers from Italy in Winter 218

To Spring 55

To Summer 123

To the Fringed Gentian 150

To Winter 210

Virtue 59

Winter 183, 223

Winter Evening 190, 230

Winter Galaxy, The 229

Winter Lakes, The.................. 186

Winter Memories 224

Winter Night, A 198

Winter Nightfall 213

Winter: My Secret 234

Winter's Song 185

Women's Harvest Song 156

Woods in Winter 188

Year's Awakening, The 20

Index of First Lines

A Bird came down the
Walk – 49

A drop fell on the apple
tree, ... 91

A late lark twitters from the
quiet skies; 167

A light exists in spring 10

A moment the wild swallows
like a flight 83

A shaded lamp and a waving
blind, ... 79

A something in a summer's
Day 68

A wrinkled crabbed man they
picture thee, ... 183

Ah, Sun-flower! weary of
time,.....................................112

...All shod with steel 194

Along the line of smoky
hills 155

Already now the snowdrop
dares appear, ... 232

Announced by all the trumpets
of the sky, ... 204

Around the house the flakes fly
faster, ... 192

Behold her, single in the
field,..................................... 139

Between the dusk of a summer
night 98

Blow, blow, thou winter wind
.... 228

Broad August burns in milky
skies, ... 96

By the purple haze that
lies 135

Calm is the morn without a
sound, ... 130

Coldly, sadly descends 162

Come live with me, and be
my love, ... 29

...Come Sons of summer, by
whose toil, ... 129

Do you ask what the birds say?
The sparrows, the dove, ... 46

Ernest and sad the solemn
tale 180

Evening, and all the birds.... 105

Fair Daffodils, we weep to
see 47

Fair summer droops, droop
men and beasts therefore, 119

Fish (fly-replete, in depth of
June) 84

Glory be to God for dappled
things – 101

Go, sit upon the lofty hill,.... 174

Gone were but the Winter, .. 44

Good-bye, good-bye to
Summer! 136

Good-night to the Season! 'tis
over!...................................... 125

Great is the sun, and wide he
goes 108

Has summer come without the
rose, ... 78

High waving heather, 'neath
stormy blasts bending, ... 202

How do you know that the
pilgrim track......................... 20

How like a winter hath my
absence been 200

How peaceable it seems for
  lonely men 14

I am waving a ripe
  sunflower, ... 156

I am Winter, that do keep 223

I bended unto me a bough of
  May, ... 25

I blow across the stagnant
  world, ... 16

I heard a thousand blended
  notes, ... 56

I know a bank whereon the wild
  thyme blows, ... 71

I leant upon a coppice gate.. 207

I love to see the old heath's
  withered brake 193

I marked the slow withdrawal
  of the year. 211

I met her in the greenest dells,
  93

I saw in Louisiana a live-oak
  growing, ... 117

I sing of brooks, of blossoms,
  birds, and bowers: 9

I sought among the drifting
  leaves, ... 168

I stood beside a hill 215

I tell my secret? No indeed,
  not I: 234

I wander'd lonely as a
  cloud 52

I'll rest me in this sheltered
  bower, ... 114

I've watched you now a full
  half-hour, ... 77

In the other gardens 142

In winter I get up at
  night 73

It is autumn; not without 177

Just now the lilac is in
  bloom, ... 121

Let the old snow be covered
  with the new: 50

Lord: it is time. The summer
  was immense 164

Loveliest of trees, the cherry
  now 32

Merry, merry sparrow! 12

My clothing was once of the
  linsey woolsey fine, ... 132

My garden blazes brightly with
  the rose-bush and the
  peach, ... 64

Nothing is so beautiful as
  spring – 35

Now came still Evening on, and
  Twilight grey 89

Now sleeps the crimson petal,
  now the white; 106

Now stir the fire, and draw the
  shutters fast, ... 190

Now that winter's gone, the
  earth hath lost 43

…Now winter nights enlarge,
  179

O Autumn, laden with fruit, and
  stained 169

O month whose promise and
  fulfilment blend, ... 99

O suns and skies and clouds of
  June, ... 170

O thou who passest thro' our
  valleys in 123

O thou with dewy locks, who
  lookest down 55

O wild West Wind, thou
  breath of Autumn's
  being; 172

'O Winter! bar thine adamantine doors:.................. 210

October's peace hath fallen on everything. 145

Oh, to be in England 63

Once more the cauldron of the sun 113

Open the window, and let the air 87

Out in a world of death far to the northward lying, ... 186

Out of the bosom of the Air,.. 197

Season of mists and mellow fruitfulness, ... 152

See what delights in sylvan scenes appear! 94

She stood breast-high amid the corn,.. 159

Sometimes a mortal feels in himself Nature 144

Spring, the sweet spring, is the year's pleasant King, ... 39

...Summer days for me, ... 67

Summer looked for long am I:.. 127

Sunned in the South, and here to-day;.................................... 218

Sweet day, so cool, so calm, so bright, ... 59

That strain again? It seems to tell 176

The day begins to droop, –.. 213

The day is cold, and dark, and dreary; 219

The day is ending, ... 216

The earth grows white with harvest; all day long 141

The glittering roofs are still with frost; each worn 201

The light rains grandly from the distant wood, ... 26

The lonely season in lonely lands, when fled 160

The meadow lark's trill and the brown thrush's whistle...... 102

The park is filled with night and fog,... 36

The poetry of earth is never dead: 72

The quiet snow 231

The roofs are shining from the rain. 24

The silver birch is a dainty lady, ... 31

The sky is silver-grey; the long 165

The soaring hawk from fist that flies, ... 220

The stars are glittering in the frosty sky, ... 229

The sun does arise, ... 40

The thistle down's flying, though the winds are all still, ... 147

The warm sun is falling, the bleak wind is wailing,........ 151

The woods that summer loved are grey and bare; 209

The year's at the spring, ... 21

There trudges one to a merry-making 148

There was a Boy; ye knew him well, ye cliffs........................ 111

They have no song, the sedges dry,... 143

Thou blossom bright with autumn dew, ... 150

Thou wilt come with suddenness, ... 11

Thou yellow trumpeter of
laggard Spring! 13

'Tis moonlight, summer
moonlight, ... 82

To make this condiment, your
poet begs 81

To-night the very horses
springing by 230

To-night the winds begin to
rise 93

Turn under, plow,.................. 182

What if the sun comes
out 33

What wondrous Life in this I
lead! 75

When biting Boreas, fell and
dour, ... 198

When daisies pied and violets
blue 22

When Icicles hang by the
wall, ... 185

When that April with his
showers sweet 19

When the clouds shake their
hyssops, and the rain 51

When the green woods laugh
with the voice of joy, ... 104

When the warm sun, that
brings 60

When winter winds are piercing
chill, ... 188

'Where shall we go for our
garlands glad 158

Within the circuit of this
plodding life......................... 224

Ye flowery banks o' bonie
Doon,..................................... 109

Yes, I remember Adlestrop—90

H. Bright